LITTLE KIDS, BIG

UESTIONS

LITTLE KIDS, BIG

UESTIONS

Practical
Answers to the
Difficult
Questions
Children Ask
About Life

Judi Craig, Ph.D.

HEARST BOOKS
NEW YORK

This book is not intended as a substitute for the help and services of a trained professional. The reader should regularly consult qualified professionals in matters relating to a child's mental or physical health and particularly to any symptoms or problems that may require diagnosis or other professional attention.

It is the policy of William Morrow and Company, Inc., and its imprints and affiliates, recognizing the importance of preserving what has been written, to print the books we publish on acid-free paper, and we exert our best efforts to that end.

Library of Congress Cataloging-in-Publication Data

Craig, Judi, 1940–
    Little kids, big questions: practical answers to the difficult
questions children ask about life / by Judi Craig, Ph.D.
        p.   cm.
    Includes index.
    ISBN 0-688-11933-6
    1. Children's questions and answers.   2. Child rearing.
I. Title.
HQ784.Q4C7   1993
649'.1—dc20   92-36928
                                                             CIP

Printed in the United States of America

A Skylight Press Book

First Edition

1   2   3   4   5   6   7   8   9   10

BOOK DESIGN BY LISA STOKES

To Sean, Tim, and Lisanne

my greatest teachers

About the Good Housekeeping Parent Guides

CHILDREN ARE A MOST WONDERFUL GIFT IN OUR LIVES—AND THEY ARE ALSO a challenge! That's why, nine years ago, we created *Good Housekeeping*'s largest-ever special editorial section: the Child Care section. Winner of a National Magazine Award in 1988, this annual section has grown by leaps and bounds to comprise more than one hundred pages, featuring articles from such notable collaborators as the American Academy of Pediatrics and the Bank Street College of Education.

THE GOOD HOUSEKEEPING PARENT GUIDES continue this spirit of helping parents meet the challenges of childrearing. Written by uniquely qualified authorities, these lively, informative books invite you to explore in-depth the everyday challenges of parenting. They are filled with ideas, examples, and strategies drawn from the real-life situations we all encounter with children. They offer new ways to understand and respond to children, as well as guidance on handling our own needs as parents.

We hope you find these guides valuable additions to your home library, providing new insights into your children, as well as innovative ideas to consider in your role as a parent. Most of all, we hope that they contribute to the loving bond you share with your child.

John Mack Carter
Editor-in-Chief
Good Housekeeping

SPECIAL THANKS TO . . .

- Meg Schneider and Lynn Sonberg of Skylight Press, for their consistency in sharpening my thinking as well as my writing! And for their talent in maintaining a perception that was always helpful and frequently amusing!

- Jim Wicoff, M.D., child and adolescent psychiatrist, colleague, and friend, for the many perceptive insights he has shared with me over the years, for his right-on suggestions for the manuscript, and for his inordinate common sense!

- Jim Norris, resident proofreader and critic, for his off-the-wall comic relief, enduring patience, and great back rubs after long hours at the word processor!

- Toni Sciarra of Hearst Books, for putting on the finishing touches!

Contents

LITTLE KIDS, BIG

UESTIONS

1

Setting the Stage

WHEN YOU LOOK AT YOUR NEWBORN LYING IN ALL HER INNOCENCE IN HER crib, you think eagerly about that day when she will look to you for your loving guidance and wisdom. You can't wait to tell her about all the wonders of life and to share with her your view of the world.

You probably plan to be more patient with her than your parents were with you. You want to take more time listening to her and answering her questions. After all, isn't being an effective teacher one of your most important jobs as a parent?

When your child is about four or five, the questions begin to fly. He wants to know why the stars stay up in the sky, why cats can't have puppies, why grass is green instead of purple. *Why* becomes his favorite word, and he's likely to be very insistent. At least these factual kinds of questions have concrete answers that you can look up in a book if you need to.

But what happens when he begins asking about feelings, relationships, God, sex, violence, motivations, values, and ethics? As a parent myself, I know how the complexity of it all can suddenly seem enormous.

You might know the answer, or think you do. But you can't figure out how to say it and have it make any sense to your child ("Why did you and Daddy stop loving each other?"). Or you may be afraid the truth will cause your youngster unnecessary anxiety ("Mommy, are you going to die?"). You might be embarrassed about the answer, thinking it's too personal ("What's an orgasm?"). Or you might feel uncomfortable about having to admit you've brought a child into a world that can be unfair or grim ("Why are there wars?").

Perhaps you haven't figured out an answer you are comfortable with ("Where is God?"). How on earth are you going to explain something to your child when you feel muddled about it yourself?

You want your child to grow up knowing she can trust you. You also need to communicate with her on her own level, but how do you begin this awesome task?

From the parents I've worked with in my twenty-six years of clinical practice, I know that parents want to communicate well with their children. When their youngsters ask questions, they don't want to blow it! What follows is a number of pointers to keep in mind so that you'll be able to communicate better with your child.

A KID'S RADAR

Psychotherapists know that if you want to find out what's really going on in a family, ask the five-year-old. She'll tell you about daddy's bad temper, mommy's headaches, and whether or not there's enough money for summer vacations.

The fact is that kids have emotional antennae. This means that if you're wondering whether your child is aware of something going on in the family—even if it hasn't been talked about openly with him—the answer is probably yes.

If you're like most parents, you're probably tempted to shield your youngster from something that's unpleasant or worrisome, in order to spare him unnecessary anxiety. You don't tell him Grandma is very sick because you're afraid he'll ask, "Is she going to die?"

Or you're walking downtown and see a homeless man ahead asking for money. Do you think your child won't figure out that you quickly crossed the street just to avoid him? What message are you really sending in your effort to be protective?

The problem is that when important information is kept from youngsters, they are stuck with worrying about it on their own. They sense that there's some secret so awful even the grown-ups can't deal with it. And they're not about to rock the boat by bringing it up!

Kids often worry unnecessarily about consequences that are far worse than what might actually happen. They hear their parents talking about the low balance in the checkbook and they jump to the conclusion they are going to wake up poor the next day. *Will we have to move out of our house? Will we have enough food to eat? Will I still get my allowance?* they might silently be asking.

If a child can feel free to go to a parent and ask about whatever is on his mind, the parent has the opportunity to correct his misgivings or, if his fear is warranted, to instruct him in appropriate ways of coping with the problem.

LITERALLY SPEAKING

The younger the child, the more likely she is to think in concrete terms. If you tell your preschooler, "Daddy's not coming home for supper because he's tied up at the office," she's likely to imagine her daddy bound and gagged at his desk chair just like on those cartoons where she sees robbers tying up their victims. If you tease her by saying, "Vanessa, I'm going to tickle you to death!" realize that she might never want to play "tickle" again!

The point is, younger children do not understand abstract thinking. For example, if you ask your four-year-old to tell you how a bicycle and a car are alike, she'll talk about wheels. An eight-year-old might say, "People ride in them." The bright preteen might tell you they both provide transportation.

In general, children from ages two to seven are unable to distinguish between internal mental states (dreaming) and external reality. They are also unable to take another person's point of view, and they tend to focus on one aspect of a situation rather than seeing the whole picture. In contrast, children from ages eight through eleven are able to use symbols to represent concrete objects (mathematical operations), can understand part-whole relationships, and can consider more than one aspect of a situation when making decisions and arriving at conclusions. They are also less egocentric, leading to the development of the capacity for empathy.

Don't think that these later cognitive abilities—such as abstraction and empathy—are locked in by the age of twelve, however. Many teens—and even adults—think primarily in concrete terms. The capacity for abstract thinking has more to do with intellect and training than with age, and teenagers are notoriously egocentric compared with most adults. Still, the beginnings of the ability to put oneself in another's place and understand the other person's position generally appears in preadolescence.

The elementary school child becomes increasingly capable of more complex thinking. The intellectually gifted child will accomplish this at an earlier age, but the process is still the same. Children begin with the literal and advance to the abstract.

MAGIC AND FANTASIES

Magicians will tell you that younger children are a more difficult audience to play for than older ones. Why? Because little kids already believe in magic. "So why shouldn't a rabbit pop out of someone's hat? What's the big deal anyway?" the five-year-old wonders as all the grown-ups are applauding.

The young child can easily believe there's a monster breathing under his bed. If you tell your child, "Honey, you don't need to worry because the monster could never get past our barking dog and our security system," he's not likely to feel comforted!

Instead parents need to tell kids that there are no monsters. There are people who dress up like monsters in the movies, and there are cameras that can take a picture of a bug and blow it up to look like a giant monster. But there are no real monsters. If your child continues to be worried about monsters after he reaches first grade, you might want to consult a mental-health professional to see why he's still having this concern.

Kids' active fantasy lives may also lead to another source of confusion in communication with adults. If a mother diapers baby sister with big brother watching and says, "You see, Allen, girls don't have penises," Allen may think that girls start out with bottoms like boys but meet with some terrible accident. If mom is unaware of this typical fantasy in children, she'll think she's giving her son a wonderful lesson in male-female anatomy, when she's actually given him something new to worry about!

ME, MYSELF, AND I

Youngsters are notoriously egocentric. This means they take everything they hear about and apply it to themselves. If they watch the news on television and hear about an earthquake on another continent, they assume that what they're seeing on the screen happened just down the block from them. If a youngster in the suburbs overhears her teachers talking about a child who was murdered in the city, she might think, "I'm next!" If the weatherman predicts snow next weekend, six-year-old Samantha might run to her closet, put on her snowsuit, and run to the door to be let outside. The young child sees everything in the here and now. She typically won't be able to tell time or to understand concepts such as today, yesterday, and tomorrow until she's seven or eight years old.

Even the older youngster continues to be egocentric in many ways.

He can hear about something on the television happening hundreds of miles away and yet maintain an expectation that the exact same thing will happen to him. Or you might tell him you're getting a divorce from his mother, and his first question might be "Who's going to give me my allowance?"

It's true that as kids grow older, they begin to learn they're not the center of the universe. There are other people out there, other families who do things differently, other children with different experiences, other religions with different practices, other countries where customs are not the same. The world broadens in scope, and the older child is better able to understand that she doesn't have to be afraid everything happening in the world is necessarily going to happen to her.

WHAT IS MY CHILD REALLY ASKING?

There's an old joke that makes a very good point. A little boy asks, "Daddy, where did I come from?" The father, playing the dutiful parent, launches into an explanation about how babies are made. Sensing his son's confusion afterward, the father asks, "What made you think of that question?" to which the boy replies, "Well, Tommy said he came from Boston and I just wanted to know where *I* came from!"

The fact is many of the questions children ask are very misleading to adults. Consequently it's important to make sure you know exactly what your child is asking before you try to answer her.

Let's say Mary asks, "Why do people kill other people?" Is she trying to understand the motivation behind murder? Is she angry at someone and is afraid she'll lose control and kill them? Or is she frightened that someone is going to kill her?

The parent who asks, "What do you think, Mary?" or "What's happened that's making you think of that question?" before answering the youngster is probably going to get more information that will help put the question in its context. That parent can then tailor the response to the child's real concern.

HOW MUCH TO TELL?

You know how frustrating it is to ask someone a question and then have him give you more information than you ever wanted to know. Children feel the same way when their parents answer them with a lecture rather than a simple, clear statement. Kids simply tune out and let the grown-up spin his verbal wheels!

In their eagerness to inform, parents often get so intent on explaining that they forget to notice if the youngster is even listening, much less understanding what is being said. They don't pick up on the child's body language, which might show puzzlement, boredom, disagreement, or even fright.

A parent who has a very bright and verbal child might begin to talk to the child as if she's older simply because she *sounds* older. To avoid this, remember to talk with your youngster at a level that's appropriate for her *chronological/emotional* age.

There's a good rule of thumb that says, "If you are not sure if you should say any more, quit talking!" Kids will readily let you know if they want more information. How? They'll simply ask another question!

Of course this won't be true if you give out an unspoken message with your own body language that you don't really want to answer a child's question in the first place. Kids sense when you are embarrassed, unsure, impatient, or unwilling to talk about the question they've asked.

To let your child know you're interested in what she has to say, make eye contact with her. If you're standing, you might even bend down so that you are at her eye level. Physical touch, such as putting your arm around her shoulder or holding her hand, can also help your child understand that you're focusing on her.

Another simple way to tell whether or not you need to give your youngster more information about a question is to ask her for feedback. "Do you understand what I mean?" is an obvious way. Even better, ask your child a question to see if she's really processing the information you've just given her. After a talk about prejudice you might say, "So now, Elizabeth, why do you suppose Jenny's mom won't let her have any black children over to play?" Elizabeth's answer will tell you if she's understood your previous explanation.

GIVING REASSURANCE

One of your most important jobs as a parent is to help your child feel safe and secure. This would be easy to do in a calm, peaceful, predictable, loving world. In the midst of today's myriad stresses, however, how do you help kids deal with all the unknowns in their lives?

Imagine you were going to be sent to another planet tomorrow. You'd be a little nervous, to say the least. You'd be wondering what the place would look like, whether the aliens would be friendly or hostile, and whether you'd be physically safe. You'd also want to know something about the habits of the aliens.

Take eating, for example. Would the aliens use some type of utensils, or would they feed themselves with their body appendages? Would they have specified times for feeding, or would they continually graze?

Now, if an interplanetary travel agent presented you with a video about the planet you'd be visiting tomorrow, chances are you'd be much less anxious about your trip after you viewed it. Why? Because you would have gotten information; you would know what to expect.

Likewise children are reassured when they are given information. They want to know what's going to happen in their immediate future. This is why you take your youngster to visit your new house before you move in, read him a book about going to the hospital before his tonsillectomy is scheduled, and tell him what to expect before he puts on roller skates for the first time.

You also convey reassurance to your child by making her world as consistent and predictable as possible. Creating some structure in her daily routine can help minimize her anxieties. Not that you have to set up a long list of rules and follow them rigidly, but there needs to be some sense of predictability. Sleeping in the same place at night, eating meals at fairly regular times, having a routine for bathing and for brushing teeth, reading a story before bedtime—these are just some of the ways you can bring a sense of security to your youngster no matter how chaotic the circumstances of your life seem at the moment.

And don't forget about discipline. Insisting that your child follow certain rules and standards of behavior, and following through with consequences when your child doesn't obey them, help your child know that you're predictable and that you can be counted on. Your discipline of your child will lead to his own self-discipline, which in turn enhances his own feelings of self-worth.

But that's not all there is to helping children feel secure. They also need words of reassurance. Even though you provide them with consistent attention and affection, they still need to hear comments like:

"I love you"
"Mommy and Daddy are always here for you"
"You're just the kind of little boy I always wanted"
"We're here to take care of you"

"We've made our house as safe as possible"
"I'll always tell you where I'm going when I leave the house"
"You can ask me any question about anything"
"I will tell you the truth"
"I'll always make sure someone is here to take care of you if I need to go someplace"
"I'll always love you, no matter what"

Realize that your child might ask for reassurance by making a negative statement. For example, she might say, "You just don't love me!" When this happens, talk to her to find out what's behind her remark. Your saying "Of course I do!" without first exploring the reasons for your child's statement can short-circuit both the extent of your reassurance and your understanding.

By giving your child verbal reassurance that you are there to care for him and that your love for him is unconditional, you help him to feel secure about his world. Whatever upsetting experiences he will encounter, he knows he can depend upon his parents. You want him to think of his home as a rock; he can venture out, but he always has that rock to come back to.

THE ART OF LISTENING

Talking is only half of communicating; equally as important is skill in listening. Sounds easy, but perceptive listening requires much more than just hearing words.

As the saying goes, "Out of the mouths of babes ..." makes the point that children can sharpen your own perception if you are willing to listen to what they have to say. Young children are direct and uninhibited, sometimes even blunt ("Mommy, your breath smells awful!"), but their point of view can be illuminating.

Why do counselors get so much more information when they listen to a child than when parents do? Probably because counselors hold back their advice and suggestions, instead making comments that invite the youngster to reveal more of her thoughts and feelings. This is called active listening.

Let's say Amy comes home from school obviously upset and announces that she's never going to speak to her best friend again. If you're like most parents, you might quickly remind her that she and this friend have been together for years, that the two of them fight all the time and then make up, that all friends fight sometimes, that she and her friend have just been spending too much time together, that she must talk to this friend again since they share the same carpool, that she's just overreacting because she didn't get enough sleep, that you've always thought her friend was a spoiled brat, that you think she's been alienating all her friends recently, that she should call up her friend immediately and try to make up, and so on. In other words, you'd interpret, analyze, make judgments, and/or give advice. It isn't that you might not be correct or have good ideas. The point is that you would jump in too fast!

But what if you simply said something like "Gosh, honey, sounds like you're pretty upset. What happened?" Amy might go on to tell you that she made a low grade on a test she studied hard for, while her friend made an A without cracking a book, and that her friend then teased her about her low grade.

Simply by curbing your impulse to console, advise, or analyze, you would now have some valuable clues about what's really troubling Amy. It might not be just a concern about friendship; her deeper issues might also be competition, unfairness, feelings of inadequacy, and/or anxiety about grades.

You could continue to explore Amy's thoughts and feelings with questions such as "How did you feel?" or "What's the part that bothers you the most?" or "What do you think you need to do next about this?" Or you might make a sympathetic remark like "Sounds pretty aggravating!" Your nonjudgmental stance allows Amy to continue ventilating until all her feelings are out in the open.

Obviously there are times when it's appropriate for you to make suggestions, offer interpretations, or give advice to your child. But try active listening first. You're likely to get much more information from your child. And you'll provide him with the opportunity to come up with his own solution to his problem. If he does, you can congratulate him for good decision making, bolstering his feelings of competence and maturity.

TUNING IN

What happens if you have one of those children who just doesn't ask many questions? First, ask yourself if you're really approachable. Does it seem like you're always in a hurry? Do you glue yourself to the television screen so that your child can only talk to you during commercials? Do you only half listen, nodding and saying "Uh-huh" when your mind is busy mulling over a problem at work and your hands are busy fixing dinner?

You don't have to be perpetually available to listen to your child.

You can say something like "Kevin, I'm thinking about something else right now and I can't really listen to you like I want to. Can we talk after supper?" Your being honest is much better than pretending to listen when your heart isn't in it. Your child gets the message that his words are important and that you are a credible listener.

It's also helpful to model open communication for your youngster. Share your feelings with her about everyday events: "Boy, it sure makes me mad when somebody tells me they're going to be here at a certain time and then they don't show up or call!" Or, "I'm feeling sad today; I just found out that my friend at work is going to be moving out of the city." Or, "My feelings got hurt when your dad forgot my birthday."

This kind of openness encourages children to feel free to express their own emotions. Of course if a parent's feelings are out of control (serious depression or anxiety), confiding feelings of such intensity can be overwhelming to a child. In that instance it would be wise for the parent to seek professional help.

Another tactic is to create opportunities for your youngster to ask you questions that you think he should be asking. If you are in the mall and your six-year-old is obviously looking at the belly of a pregnant woman, you might remark, "Julie, that woman is going to have a baby soon. Do you know how babies get born?" Or if a television show depicts a youngster telling another child that he feels guilty because he thinks he caused his parents' divorce, you might ask, "Bobby, do you ever wonder if Mom and I got divorced because of something you did?"

By seizing those appropriate moments that arise spontaneously, you can educate your youngster about issues or concerns you think might apply to him. You can also arrange times away from home when you and your child can talk without any intrusions. Riding in the car, taking your child to breakfast or lunch, or going for a walk provide ideal times for such conversation. Also realize that children's defenses are down at the end of the day, so bedtime is often a good time to talk things over. Finding good times to initiate a talk can lighten the burden on the child who might be too shy, anxious, or embarrassed to bring up something that bothers him.

A LITTLE FEAR?

Sometimes you have to walk a tight line as a parent: you have to caution your child about all sorts of dangers in the world, but you have to do it in a way that doesn't give him nightmares and deep anxiety! When it comes to electric sockets, busy streets, and strangers offering candy, you don't want to be permissive about your child's involvement.

If your young child is heading for danger, you want to do whatever you can to stop him immediately. A loud, firm "No, Shannon!" and removal from the source of the danger, perhaps even with a brief swat on the behind to make the point, gives a very clear message. While corporal punishment is not recommended in general, this is the type of situation in which the immediate negative reinforcement serves a good purpose.

But how do you tell your child that there are people in the world who try to harm children without making her afraid of everyone she meets? The warning "Don't ever talk to a stranger!" doesn't send an accurate message. After all, if your child is in the supermarket and a woman she doesn't know compliments her or says, "Hello," you probably want your child to respond appropriately.

Rather than telling her not to speak to strangers, let your youngster know that she should never get in a car, go into a house, or go anywhere with someone—even if she recognizes the person—without your permission. Explain in a calm, matter-of-fact manner that there are some adults who try to hurt children and that these adults often act very friendly to a child to get that child to go somewhere with them. Sometimes these adults try to tempt kids with bribes (such as toys, candy, or the promise of seeing some baby kittens, etc.), so warn your youngster about these tricks.

After you tell your child this information, follow it up by saying something like "Honey, most adults are very nice people and would never try to hurt a child. I just wanted to tell you about not going with someone unless Dad or I have told you it's okay, just in case you would happen to run into a person who tries to hurt kids. It's always best not to take chances; that way you'll be safe."

While it's unpleasant to have to discuss things like this with your child, it's a necessity in today's world. If your child becomes preoccupied with fears about adults who try to harm children after you discuss this topic with him, there are probably other sources of anxiety underneath this issue. Consultation with a mental-health professional is recommended.

A TOUGH JOB

Being a parent in today's world is not easy. Family structures are no longer static, values are continually being reassessed, and the world is changing dramatically. What is predictable is the lack of predictability!

There is no definitive book, video, course, or point of view that can tell you how to be a good parent, much less provide any guarantee that your child will turn out to be a well-adjusted, happy, and productive citizen. So it's pointless to expect yourself to have all the answers or to handle every situation that comes up with your child in a "perfect" way.

Television, although it has many positive educational aspects, can also make parenting more difficult. Its emphasis on materialism, sexuality, and instant gratification sets up unrealistic expectations for youngsters, and the violence that fills the screen requires a great deal of parental monitoring, especially for the young child.

Due to the social and environmental pressures that were absent thirty years ago, being a good parent today means being able to guide your youngster through a myriad of concepts and values that might be quite foreign to your own way of thinking. Because you also might be experiencing stress from today's pressures, as you go through this journey, remember to be gentle with yourself.

WHAT'S COMING UP

In the chapters that follow you'll find typical questions kids ask about a variety of important life issues. The questions are grouped into categories (love, death, sex, etc.) for easy reference and are asked in the words kids are likely to use.

When several interpretations of what the child is really asking are possible, each will be addressed. When the answers are different for younger (ages four to seven) and older (ages eight to twelve) youngsters, explanations for both will be given.

After each question you'll find examples of related questions that touch on the same issues. These are given for easy reference in case you're looking to see if your child's particular slant on a question is answered in that section.

Along with information about the topics you'll need to cover in answering your youngster's questions, you'll find a liberal sprinkling of examples of appropriate responses. These aren't meant to be followed to the letter, but sometimes it just seems to help to have some actual responses in mind. The sample answers might help you feel more comfortable in your dialogue with your child.

Although you might plan to use this book to look up a specific topic of concern to you and your child, I recommend that you read it all the way through the first time, even if you think that some chapters or questions would never apply to you. I've attempted to convey a certain style and attitude that I think are helpful when you talk to kids. The examples provided throughout the book might help you develop a more meaningful and more relaxed way of interacting with your child.

Readers of my parenting column, as well as parents who consult me in my office, have assisted me greatly in knowing what kinds of questions are difficult for parents to answer. I hope you'll find your specific concerns in the chapters that follow.

2
Friendship/Love

KIDS HAVE A PRETTY GOOD IDEA OF WHAT FRIENDSHIP IS. IT'S OTHER KIDS talking to them, laughing with them, and including them in their play. When they ask what love is, however, things can get a little tricky!

Your simplest answer can be "Love is when you care about someone." At some point, however, you're going to have to explain that there are many different kinds of love. You love your kids differently than you love your mate, your own parents, your friends, or the people on the other side of the world.

The important thing to a child of course is that you love him. You want to reassure him that you will always love him unconditionally, no matter what. In other words you'll still love him even if he's making F's, making a mess in his pants, shouting at you, writing notes with dirty words to his friends, taking money out of your wallet without permission, refusing to brush his teeth, or doing any of a number of things that tend to drive parents up the wall!

Why is your unconditional love so important to him? Because feeling that he is lovable is the basis of his self-worth. You want your child to feel in his gut that his essence as a human being is special, unique, and inherently wonderful no matter what his behavior might be like at the moment.

A child also needs your encouragement to love himself. Not in a narcissistic, self-centered, egotistical way but in a manner that demonstrates a healthy respect for his own humanness and imperfection. Mistakes are simply lessons. The goal is to learn from them, not to use them to beat up on himself.

As your child gets older, you'll want to teach her that genuine, mature love between two people is not the same thing as the typical romantic love so often depicted on television and in the movies. Genuine love is freeing, not possessive or controlling. It doesn't demand that the loved one change to suit someone else. Instead love is based on mutual respect for each person's feelings.

You'll also want to let your older youngster know that love is not just a feeling. It's an attitude, a choice. He can choose to behave in a loving way or he can choose not to. If he's aggravated by his friend's behavior, he doesn't have to have a temper tantrum or be rude. He can choose to give his friend the benefit of the doubt, forgive him, and continue being pleasant and sociable.

You want your child to understand that friendship is one expression of love. She'll want good things to happen to her friend, she won't want to do anything to hurt her friend, she'll want to be there for her friend during the happy and the not-so-happy times, she'll want to let her friend know she still cares even when her friend does something she doesn't like. The attitude of friendliness, harmlessness, and nonjudgment then becomes a model for loving all people throughout the world.

You'll also want to help your child realize why loving is so important. Love is unique because it not only helps the one being loved, it also helps the one doing the loving. Love is contagious and comes back to you. To love is to feel good about yourself, about other people, and about everything around you. It is like a gift—it makes you feel good whether you give it or receive it.

1. WHY DOESN'T ANYBODY LIKE ME?
   What's wrong with me?
   Why do kids always pick on me?

Probably the first decision you'll need to make before answering this question is whether or not your child is perceiving the situation accurately. Do her peers really reject her, or does she actually have quite a few friends? Is she perhaps overreacting to being snubbed by one particular youngster or to being teased in one social situation? Careful listening will help you decide.

QUESTION MOTIVATED BY ACTUAL SOCIAL REJECTION

You know how important it is for a child to feel well liked, and your heart aches for her if she is being rejected by her peers. What's even more frustrating is your sense of helplessness because you can't control the situation. Since most of your child's interaction with other kids happens without your being present to see exactly what's going on, sometimes you really don't have any idea what the trouble is. More often, though, you do sense what's happening, either from your own observations or from reports of teachers and other adults.

Your child typically will deny her contribution to the difficulty. All problems are the other kid's fault, and if you try to point out something to her that she could do differently, she may have an endless list of excuses about why your suggestions won't work.

One way around this dilemma is to discuss what kids do that makes other kids like them. Ask your child what she thinks popular kids do that makes them popular. Or you might say, "Debbie, who's the most popular, well-liked girl in your class? What does she do that gets the other kids to like her so much?"

If your daughter's response is "Erica. Because she gives candy to everyone," or, "Because she's pretty and everybody loves her," reassure her that kids who try to buy popularity or who gain friends because of their good looks are not really gaining true friendship. Such children might be momentarily popular for these superficial reasons, but they will not keep friends unless they develop other qualities that sustain friendship.

If your child tells you some things Erica does that you consider to be appropriate, encourage her to do the same. Help her understand that it's not that Erica is perfect, either, but she might be a good example of someone with good social skills. Then encourage her to act friendly. This means talking to other kids, smiling at them, and being willing to share.

If this tactic doesn't work, you might try a more indirect approach. Ask your child to tell you the things kids do that make other kids *not* like them. "Jenny, tell me some things your classmates do that you don't like?" or, "What are some things other kids do that make you not like them?" Some youngsters love the more imaginative "inside out" approach: "Let's pretend you're going to teach a class to kids who want other kids to dislike them. What would you tell them to do to make sure nobody would ever want to play with them again?"

Together you and your child can make a list of these behaviors. The list might include entries like:

> Bosses people around
> Acts like a crybaby

Won't take turns
Doesn't follow rules
Hits people
Brags all the time
Makes fun of other kids
Won't share toys
Steals other kid's things
Calls people names
Tattles
Kicks, spits, shoves, pinches
Too goodie-goodie
Can't take a joke
Knows all the answers
Acts like teacher's pet

By making this list, you decrease your child's defensiveness about acknowledging her part in the problem, since it's highly unlikely that she's doing every one of these things. Now she can feel good about all those negative things she *doesn't* do!

At this point ask your youngster to look over the list and tell you which of these things she's done. If she denies them all, gently remind her of an instance you recall or heard about from a reliable source. Once she's admitted an action, you can ask, "Well, honey, what could you do instead?" and then help her design a plan.

If your child is having problems because he's become the brunt of teasing, explain that he must develop a different way to respond when he's teased. He can't stop the bully from bullying, but he can change his reaction to the bullying. He needs to understand that if he cries, runs away, or has a temper fit, the bully has won.

The standard advice of "Just ignore it!" might not work, although it's a good tactic to try at first. Obviously it's no fun to tease someone who won't give you the satisfaction of a reaction. But a child who's repeatedly teased will usually have to develop a more assertive strategy.

"Cut it out!" or, "Grow up!" or, "Yeah! Right!" are often effective responses, followed by the child's walking away if possible. Sometimes saying "Does it really make you feel good to try to hurt my feelings?" will work. The trick is for your child to act matter-of-fact, no matter what the bully does.

Suggest your child hang out with kids who like her. There's safety in numbers, and a youngster who's alone is a more vulnerable victim for a teaser. Friends will sometimes make a remark to the bully on the victim's behalf, giving the victim the necessary support to remain unruffled.

2. IF I PLAY WITH NANCY, SUZANNE WON'T PLAY WITH ME ANYMORE. WHAT SHOULD I DO?

When your child has a friend who's threatening to withdraw her friendship if your youngster is friends with someone else, explain to your child that this friend is trying to control her. This tactic is emotional blackmail, plain and simple. The child making such a statement is using her so-called friendship as a weapon to get your youngster to do what she wants. Make this clear to your child and ask her if that's what she wants in a friend.

The trouble is, your child is fearful of losing this friend. Perhaps the friend has high status among her peers, and your youngster is worried that her peer group will reject her if she goes against the wishes of this leader. Or perhaps the two girls have been close friends for a long time and your child would be genuinely sad to lose this relationship. Or your child might be afraid to lose this friendship for fear she'll never make another friend.

If you suspect that Suzanne is issuing this order because she's insecure and feels threatened by your child's having another friend, suggest to your youngster that she reassure Suzanne she'll continue to be friends with her also. If Suzanne refuses to accept this situation, then that's Suzanne's choice.

For an older child you might teach her to say something like "Suzanne, let me see if I understand what you want me to do. You mean that if I'm your friend, then I can't be friends with anybody else?" Confronting Suzanne with this question may help her see the ridiculousness of her request.

If you suspect that Suzanne's threat has something to do specifically with Nancy (she's too smart, too nasty, dresses funny, smells bad, etc.), suggest to your child that she explain to Suzanne that she wants to be friendly to everyone. "It's unfair to be unfriendly to someone just because she does some things you might not like," or, "Everybody needs friends; it will hurt Nancy's feelings if I won't be her friend."

Your child might protest that Suzanne really will reject her if she insists on befriending Nancy. At this point reassure your child that kids who don't allow their affections to be swayed by other people and remain true to their own feelings end up being trusted and well liked. Although she might lose Suzanne's friendship right now, she'll

probably regain it. Even if she doesn't and even if other peers temporarily turn away because of her decision, she'll be a winner in the
long run because her peers will realize that she's a true friend. Even
more important she'll feel good about being in control of her own
decisions and standing up for what she thinks is right.

Tell your child that a person cannot allow herself to be manipulated
by a fear of rejection by other people. Sometimes that means she
just can't be friends with everybody, but she can remain friendly to
everybody.

3. I LIKE JANE. WHY DOESN'T JANE LIKE ME?
   If someone doesn't like me, did I do something wrong?
   How can I make Peter like me?
   Why can't I be more popular?

When a youngster wants to be friends with another child who spurns
her, hurt feelings are in store. It's even hard for adults to accept the fact
that someone might not like them, whatever the reason.

If you think your child is being rejected because of something he
or she is doing, see Question 1. But if it's one of those unexplainable
matters of individual preference, explain to your youngster that it's
irrational to expect everyone to like you. Let her know that nobody
can be liked by everybody, and it doesn't mean that she's a bad person
if someone rejects her.

You might say, "I don't know why that little girl doesn't like you,
honey. Sometimes people are just like that, and you can't do anything
about it. It doesn't mean there's anything wrong with you."

Remind your child of a peer she's never wanted to make friends
with, pointing out that other kids do like that particular child. It's all
a matter of preference. Then point out to her the friends she does
have to let her know that she's likable.

If you think there's something specific your child could do to try
to gain the other youngster's friendship, give her your suggestions.
"Have you invited her to come over and play after school?" or, "Have
you tried sharing a goodie from your lunch box?" or, "Have you asked
her to show you how to do something she does well?" But make it
clear that when it comes right down to it, you can't force another
person to like you.

You can also give your youngster some general suggestions to help
her be well liked by her peers. Believe it or not, simply smiling when
she talks will help your child appear friendly. So will giving sincere
compliments to her peers. Being a good listener is also a key, as all

of us feel comfortable talking to someone who knows when to be quiet and just listen.

When your child is rejected, asking "How does that make you feel?" might help her get her hurt or angry feelings out in the open. If she denies having any feelings about the situation, you can tell her, "Well, if someone I liked didn't like me back, it would hurt my feelings." Once your child admits her feelings, reassure her by telling her the many reasons why other kids do like her.

Realize, however, that you don't always have to talk to your child to comfort her. Sometimes words seem to interfere, and just being there in silence with her—perhaps holding her hand or putting your arm around her—can be a powerful way to show your support.

Don't give in to the temptation to express your shock or indignation about this other child's not liking your youngster. To do so just makes a mountain out of a molehill. Instead give your youngster a clear message that this sort of thing is to be expected from time to time and, though hurtful, should be casually accepted.

Explain to your child that popularity is not the proper goal. Even if it were, a person can do everything conceivable to try to be accepted by others and still be rejected. Being a good, reliable friend who can be trusted to stand up for her true beliefs is what really matters. The youngster who is able to do this consistently will not have to worry about having friends in the long run.

4. WHY SHOULD I BE NICE TO MARK IF HE'S NOT NICE TO ME?
   Johnny says he hates me. Why do I have to keep being nice to him?

This question provides you with a wonderful opportunity to teach your child that two wrongs do not make a right! Better yet, you get the chance to teach him the value of being the kind of person he wants to be without being swayed by other people.

For a young child you might say, "Honey, it's best to be polite to Mark when you see him. But I'd try to stay away from him if you can. Just don't play near him if you can help it." You might even add, "You know, Mark might be mean because he's an unhappy boy. But it still doesn't help for you to be mean back to him." Or you might ask him, "Ricky, what would happen if every time someone was grumpy around here, I'd be grumpy right back? Wouldn't be a very fun house to live in, would it?"

With an older youngster you can talk about the fact that a person's self-worth increases when he behaves in ways that mesh with his own values. A person feels good when he doesn't give in to the negativity of other people. He stands up for what he believes in, which is friendliness and compassion toward everyone.

The older child might also begin to understand the concept of brotherhood: "It will never be a peaceful world if people are always ready to be nasty to people who don't agree with them."

Let your child know that each individual has an opportunity to change the attitudes of those around him by his own example. You might point out an instance when someone in the family was in a grouchy mood but cheered up when the other family members remained loving and cheerful. Ask him to imagine how things would have gone if the other people in the family had become grouchy as well.

It's also helpful to point out that people have reasons for not always being nice to others that have nothing to do with the person they are mistreating. If a child walks into the classroom and the teacher snaps at him, "Take your seat!" the youngster doesn't have to take it personally. Maybe the teacher just got some bad news; maybe she didn't get enough sleep the night before; maybe someone in her family is sick and she's worried about him; maybe she has a headache.

By suggesting that a youngster consider what motivates a person whose behavior seems negative or unfriendly, you teach him to be sensitive to the feelings and circumstances of others. That doesn't mean of course that he has to "take" the mistreatment of the negative party; he might want to tell the other child that he's being grumpy or complaining. But the point is that your child learn that he's in control of his own moods and behavior. He doesn't have to let another person turn him into the kind of person he doesn't really want to become.

You might also teach your child how to invite the other youngster to change. Suggest he say something like "Hey, you seem pretty mad at me. What's the problem? Why don't we talk about it?" This suggestion helps your child learn the beginnings of conflict resolution at an early age.

5. WHO DO YOU LOVE THE MOST, ME OR MY SISTER?
   Why do you pay more attention to him? Do you love him more?

If you're a typical parent, your off-the-top-of-the-head answer would be "Honey, I love you both the same!" But think again.

Imagine if you asked your mate, "Honey, who do you love more, your mother or me?" and he answered, "Honey, I love you both the same!" would you feel wonderful and fulfilled by his answer? It's doubtful!

The point is it's simply not reassuring or comforting to feel you're lumped together with anyone else when it comes to love. Kids feel the same way. They want to know they're special to you and that nobody else could ever replace them.

So you could say, "Honey, you are my one and only Lisa! There's nobody else in the world like you, and I love you with all my heart for being YOU! Your sister is my one and only Pam, and I love her for being Pam. There's just no way to ever compare the two of you."

At this point tell your child some qualities or talents she has that make her special. Mention some things she's done or said that are dear to your heart and that you'll always remember about her. By the end of this conversation she'll feel special and truly loved.

If your child complains that you love his brother or sister more, allow him to tell you all the reasons why he thinks this is true. Even if his examples sound trivial to you, listen anyway. If explanations are in order, give them.

Then reassure your youngster that you do love him. Tell him why he's special to you and that there's not another person in the world like him. You might end the conversation by saying something like "Now, whenever you're feeling unloved or wondering about it, I want you to come to me and tell me so we can talk about it. Okay?" This gives your child a sense of security in knowing he can always ask for your reassurance.

It's also helpful to explain to your children that you'll probably never pay equal attention to each of them at all times. The truth is situations occur when one child needs more attention from his parents than at other times. For instance you'll obviously give more attention to a youngster who's sick than to one who isn't. Other examples include times when one child is having difficulty in school, is having a crisis with a friend, or is involved in some legal trouble.

Realize that children often equate amounts of attention with amounts of love. To help them see the difference, you might say, "Honey, attention is like a pie—there's only so much to go around. Sometimes you get a big piece and sometimes you get a little piece. But love isn't split up into pieces; it's *always* there, just like the air we breathe."

6. IF YOU LOVE ME, HOW COME YOU WON'T LET ME DO IT?
How can you ground me if you love me?
If you love me, why won't you let me do what Susie's mother lets her do?

Your answer to this question depends on whether your child is asking it because she's misbehaved and is in trouble or because she's trying to win permission to do what she wants.

QUESTION MOTIVATED BY MISBEHAVIOR

If a kid has one trick that's most likely to get a grown-up to reduce a punishment, it's to try to make the adult feel guilty. What better way to do this than to accuse that adult of not loving her?

When faced with this manipulative ploy, many parents will launch into a lengthy discussion about all the things they do and have done for that child to show their love: "Didn't I just let you have a friend spend the night, take you roller-skating, buy you ice cream, and even let you buy those pretty ponytail holders?" Or, tearfully, "After all those ballet lessons I've driven you to, all the times I've made cookies for your class, all those nights I sat up with you when you had tummy problems, all those times I've not bought something for me so I could buy nice clothes for you, how could you even think such a thing?"

When your child hits you with this form of manipulation, refocus her attention on the real issue: "Tiffany, we're not talking about love right now. We're talking about the fact that you brought this note from the teacher telling me you haven't been turning in your assignments."

You can also quickly dismiss you child's accusation with "Sam, you know that's ridiculous! Now, how did you talk yourself into taking money out of my purse?"

QUESTION MOTIVATED BY SEEKING PERMISSION

Kids often want permission to do something you consider inappropriate. You might think they're too young or that what they want to do is dangerous or goes against your moral values. Or you might feel that they're old enough by usual standards but that they're not yet ready to use good judgment in the situation.

Let your child know that part of your job of being a good parent is to use your judgment about what's best for her. She might be unhappy with your decision, but your goal is not her constant happiness. Explain that sometimes the most loving thing a parent can do is to make a decision that is unpopular with the child. Your primary goal is her physical safety and her emotional development, not her approval: "Adrianna, I'm sorry you think I'm unfair on this. I simply will not allow you to ride your bike to your friend's house after dark. It's too dangerous."

Children will sometimes bring in outside influences to bolster their position: "Well, Susie's mom lets her have a dog. If you loved me, you'd let me have one too!" Again, refocus the child's attention on the issue rather than the question of love. "I'm not letting you get a dog because your dad is allergic to animals. It doesn't have anything to do with love."

Sometimes it's helpful to use an exaggerated example to make your point: "Honey, I love you so much, I wish I could get you a hundred dogs, but you know your dad is allergic to them. I'm sorry."

The point is not to become emotional over your child's accusation that you don't love him. To do so only demonstrates your fear your child might be right—you're not as loving a parent as you might want to be.

7. IF YOU AND DADDY LOVE EACH OTHER, WHY DO YOU FIGHT?
If you love me, why do you yell at me?
If Mommy loves me, why does she get mad at me so much?

You want your child to understand that people who love each other do get mad at each other. It's perfectly normal. After all, if you didn't care so much about the other person, you wouldn't waste the energy it takes to be angry and try to work things out.

For the younger child it might be enough to say, "Honey, your dad and I fight sometimes, but we love each other very much." All he wants to hear is simple reassurance that the security of the family is not in danger.

The older youngster is probably ready for some lessons in interpersonal relations: "Honey, you got real mad at me this morning when I wouldn't fix you a waffle. But I know you still love me, right? It's the same way with your dad and me, or any two people who care about each other. They're going to disagree and get angry, maybe even fight for a while. It's part of learning to be honest with one another. You can't live with someone and not ever get mad at them. If you hold your anger in and don't talk about it, you end up with worse problems. When you talk it out, even if you're loud about it, you have a chance to work things out so that both people can feel better."

Sometimes kids wonder how you can love them and still yell at them. Again, they need to hear that anger is a natural emotion that needs to be released in an appropriate way. It would be nice never to yell, but yelling is a lot better than throwing things around or hitting people.

You can also use an analogy to make your point. Ask your child to pretend he has a deflated balloon in his chest. Have him imagine that every time he feels angry about something, the balloon expands a bit. Eventually the balloon gets so big from stuffing those angry feelings that it bursts. It simply can't handle any more anger without exploding.

Explain that people are a lot like those balloons. If you stuff your angry feelings instead of releasing them when they're fresh, you end up exploding. Then even one little thing going wrong can be enough to break the whole balloon!

Although you need to teach your child that anger needs to be expressed, make sure he understands you're not giving him permission to go wildly out of control when he's mad. There are appropriate ways of showing anger that are not severely intimidating, threatening, or dangerous to other people.

When children are taught that anger is perfectly normal, they don't think of it as interfering with love. They can even learn that it's healthy for two people who care about each other to show their angry feelings to each other.

8. IF PARENTS LOVE THEIR CHILDREN, WHY IS THERE CHILD ABUSE?
   How can Terry's dad say he loves him when he does awful things to Terry?

Since child abuse is often talked about in the media, kids are all too aware that it occurs. Chances are they might hear about a child in their school who is abused, or they might have a friend who tells them she's being abused by a parent. Naturally they wonder how such a thing can happen when all parents supposedly love their children.

For a young child answer this question as simply as possible: "Honey, Terry's dad must be very troubled. I'm sure he loves Terry, but for some reason he can't control his temper." Explain that parents who have this kind of problem can go to people who will help them stop hurting their children.

An older youngster will want more explanation. Tell her that child abuse occurs because some adults lose control of their anger. This happens for a variety of reasons: The parent might be mentally ill or have an alcohol or drug problem. Or the parent might suffer from emotional problems or have trouble controlling his impulses, especially in times of stress or family or money problems. In such cases frustration builds, and the parent inappropriately releases anger on the child.

Let your child know that most parents who abuse their children do actually love those children and feel terribly guilty after they have hurt them. Many of these parents were victims of abuse themselves when they were little and carry an inner rage that can be easily triggered when they are severely frustrated. Since their own parents modeled violence for them, their first response is to do the same thing with their children, unless they have learned some specific techniques to release their anger in less harmful ways. These parents lose control, but they don't stop loving their kids.

What if this abuse issue comes closer to home and your child is asking this question because he or a sibling has experienced an abusive incident by you or your spouse? Admit the problem exists and apologize to your child for what happened. Reassure him of your love and tell him that you (or your spouse) are going to a professional for help with this problem.

9. DO PEOPLE LOVE EACH OTHER FOREVER?
   If I do something bad, will you stop loving me?
   Will Tim still love me after he leaves home?
   Will Cindy and I always be friends?

It's a good idea to find out what prompted this question before you answer it. Is your child afraid that you will stop loving her? Or is she worried that you and your mate will stop loving one another? Does she fear that her big brother who's going off to college won't love her anymore after he leaves home? Or is she worried about losing the friendship of someone special?

QUESTION MOTIVATED BY FEAR THAT PARENT WILL STOP LOVING CHILD

Kids want reassurance that their parents will always love them forever, no matter what. They need to experience this unconditional love in order to feel secure and lovable. But they wonder, "What if Mommy knew that I wish my baby sister would go back to heaven?"

or, "What if I flunk third grade?" They worry that their parents will quit loving them because they have done or thought about something they consider to be bad.

Reassure your youngster about this very directly. "Honey, no matter what you ever do, I will always love you," or, "There's nothing you could ever do or think of doing that would make me stop loving you, Jerry."

Your child might ask this question because you've disciplined her or because she's done something she's feeling guilty about. Let her know that you might not approve of certain behaviors, but that this has nothing to do with loving her: "Maggie, I don't like your hitting your brother and I had to discipline you for it. But that doesn't mean I don't love you." Keep this explanation matter-of-fact, however; you don't want your child to think you're apologizing for disciplining her by deluging her with hugs, kisses, and extra attention.

QUESTION MOTIVATED BY CHILD'S FEAR ABOUT DIVORCE

When your youngster learns there's such a thing as divorce, he'll realize there are situations in which people start out loving each other but change their minds. Admit that adults don't always love each other forever, but that parents always love their kids forever: "Jenny's parents don't love each other anymore the way married people are supposed to love each other, but Jenny's parents will always love Jenny" (see Chapter 4 for more information about divorce).

QUESTION MOTIVATED BY FEAR OF LOSING LOVE OF A RELATIVE

When a brother or sister leaves home, the child who's left might worry that the older sibling will forget all about him. The closer the two have been, the greater the feeling of loss. Especially if the young adult moves away or doesn't keep much contact with little brother, the younger child may worry that the older one doesn't love him anymore. The same problem will exist when any loved relative moves out of the child's house.

Explain to your child that distance doesn't destroy love when there's a strong bond, as there is between family members: "Bradley, my sister lives far away and I only see her once every couple of years. But we will always love each other, and we stay close by talking on the phone and writing letters."

Or, "Mary's very busy with her new life at college, but don't think for a moment that she doesn't still love you. Why don't you write her a letter, or maybe we can call her on Sunday?" Or, "Honey, kids grow up and start lives of their own, but they don't stop loving their families. You two will have a lot to talk about when Eric comes home to visit."

Although you want your child to know that the family member will still love her after he's moved, let her know that you realize there is a loss involved: "I know you feel sad about Grandpa moving back to California, Stacy. It hurts to see someone you love go far away," or, "I know it's going to be different around here without Max banging on his guitar and bugging you about your freckles. I bet you're feeling kind of sad about his leaving home next week."

QUESTION MOTIVATED BY FEAR OF LOSING A FRIENDSHIP

Kids can easily see that even "best friends" break up. But when it's *their* best friend, it's very common for them to imagine that their friendship will last forever. The bond is so strong they can't imagine anything coming between them. If trouble begins between them or if they see a split between another pair of best friends, it might be hard for them to understand how such a thing could happen.

Explain to your child that friendships are precious but that they might in fact not last forever. People change, and sometimes people grow apart because of those changes. Take two girls who enjoyed playing dolls and having tea parties when they were eight. At age ten one might still be into the same kind of play; the other might mature more quickly and want nothing to do with what she now considers child's play. Since the two girls now differ in their level of maturity, they are unlikely to remain close.

Let your youngster know that the same thing can happen with adult friendships. People continue to grow emotionally throughout their lifetime, often leaving behind friends with whom they once had much in common.

Tell your child that circumstances can also cause friends to grow apart. It's hard to stay close to a classmate who changes schools or moves out of town. Adults are more likely to remain friends with people they haven't seen in years; kids generally lose touch with one another unless they physically share similar activities.

When your child is anticipating the ending of an important friendship, recognize the fact that she's dealing with a loss. She will feel sad, perhaps even scared about whether or not she'll ever find such another good friend. Explain the reasons why you think the friendship is breaking up and give her permission to grieve: "Honey, you and Ellen have been going in different directions for the last few months. She's really so involved with her gymnastics now, it's only natural she's becoming good friends with the other girls on the team. You two have very different interests. I know you feel sad about her not calling you much anymore; it's really hard to lose a good friend."

Encourage your youngster to look around her peer group for kids involved in the same activities as she is and to begin to seek their friendship: "You know that girl you like on your basketball team? Why don't you invite her over this weekend?" or, "Look at the other fourth-graders tomorrow and pick out a couple of girls you'd like to know better; then strike up a conversation with them."

MORE SUGGESTIONS

1. For a young child who's continuing to have problems making or keeping friends in spite of your talking with her about the reasons, try puppet play to get your point across. Let your youngster "be" the puppet who's the bully or the teaser so that you get a better idea of what she's experiencing, then role-play your child, making appropriate responses. Switch roles to help your child practice different response strategies, and repeat this process until she's more confident in her social skills.

For an older youngster simply role-play without using puppets. Take turns playing the roles, perhaps exaggerating the drama to keep it fun for both of you.

2. To help a child feel truly loved, give him sincere compliments that don't depend on his having done something to earn them. "Honey, you're just the kind of little boy I always wanted"; "I love having you around because you're such good company"; "I'm so glad you're you"; "You know, it's really fun having you for a kid." By focusing on his essence rather than his behavior, you'll strengthen his feeling that you love him unconditionally.

3. The power of touch can never be underestimated. Give your child a liberal dose of affectionate hugs and pats. Make sure, of course, that they're the kind he likes (he might not like having his hair touseled; she might feel that your holding her hand is babyish).

3
Sex

IT USED TO BE OKAY NOT TO TELL YOUR KIDS ABOUT SEX. NOBODY TALKED about it much, at least not openly. If it was talked about, it was often made to seem secretive or even slightly "dirty."

Then along came feminism, sexual freedom, and a sexuality blitz from the media. Talk shows thrive on it, "sex experts" write books about it, and sitcoms and soaps sell it. And if you want little left to your imagination, just turn on your cable television.

Facing all of this calmly means that as a parent you are now forced to face your own sexuality. It's not hard to see your own hang-ups if you have any; but whether you do or not, you probably don't want your kids to have them. You realize that what you do or don't tell your youngster about sex can greatly affect her future sexual functioning. Not only that but you don't want your child to get her sex education from the wrong sources.

Your dilemma might be "I want to tell my child about sex, but I just don't know when it's the right time." A very good rule of thumb is to answer his question at the time he asks it. Or when he reacts nonverbally in such a way that you know he's wondering about it. Typically kids are ready for basic information long before parents think they are. Putting your youngster off with "I'll tell you when you're older" is a cop-out.

Youngsters will generally ask about sexual anatomy as toddlers. Where babies come from and how they are born is often a topic of concern to four- and five-year-olds. Questions about sexual intercourse usually come up anywhere between age five up through the elementary school years. Puberty issues, such as breast development and wet dreams, need to be discussed before a child enters that phase of development. Since over twenty-five percent of girls will begin to menstruate between the ages of ten and twelve, you can see that puberty might need to be discussed with a girl as early as the fourth grade. Although concerns about the decision to become sexually active don't usually surface until the teen years, many older elementary school children will ask when they will be old enough to start having sex.

You might wonder which parent is the best one to talk to the child about sex. A common assumption is that mothers should tell girls and fathers should tell boys.

In fact it really doesn't make any difference who tells whom. Young children will most likely ask the parent who helps them with dressing, toileting, and bathing. Older children will usually go to the parent who's most comfortable discussing sexual matters.

Your most uncomfortable moments when your child asks something about sex will probably occur if your youngster personalizes her question: "Mommy, do you and Daddy do that?" "When did you first have sex?" "Can I see your vagina?" Kids can be so direct that they startle an unsuspecting parent who's trying to tell her child the facts of life.

When this happens, make it clear that you'll give your child any information he asks for in a general sense, but that you won't allow an invasion of your privacy: "Mark, that is really nobody's business but Daddy's and mine. Sex is a very private matter between two people who love each other," or, "Honey, that's a private part of my body. I'll be happy to show you a picture of how a woman's bottom looks, though."

Remember, your child has a vivid imagination. Since sex is a complicated subject, his fantasies about it have room to run rampant. What he imagines can carry far more weight that what he's actually told.

For this reason respond to your child's question about sex by first asking him what he *thinks* the answer is. This approach will show you what he does and doesn't understand.

For instance consider a common kid's fantasy about pregnancy. Many young children see the large belly of a pregnant woman and assume she ate something that made a baby grow inside her stomach. This same child might take this a step farther and be frightened to go have a bowel movement for fear that a baby will pop out!

Another point to remember is that children often find sexual information shocking or even disgusting: "You mean you and Dad had to do *that* to have me? Yuck!" Because the anatomy for sex and the anatomy for bathroom functions are in such close proximity, youngsters often react with disdain when they understand specific sexual behaviors.

If this happens when you're discussing sex with your child, you might say something like "Well, honey, I felt the same way when I was your age. But you'll probably change your mind when you're older and will understand all this better." This message communicates your understanding of where your child is coming from, gives her permission to change her mind, and lets her know that you don't consider sex to be negative or disgusting.

It's also important not to overwhelm your child with too much information. "That's called a tampon" might be all she needs to hear. If she asks what it's for, you might tell her, "It's a piece of cotton I use." She'll let you know if she really wants to know more.

Your goal is to help your child feel comfortable with his sexuality. This requires more than just giving out correct factual information about sexual anatomy and functions. It also requires teaching a perspective about the role of sexuality in a person's life. While you could limit that perspective to the idea that sex exists solely for the purpose of reproduction, you might want to instill the view that sexuality offers a valuable and joyful channel for the expression of deep intimacy between two people who love and care for each other.

1. MOMMY, HOW COME I DON'T HAVE A PENIS?
   Which is better, a penis or a vagina?
   Why is my penis so little?

Even very young children are aware of and curious about their bodies. They notice that the world is divided into people called boys and people called girls, and they're quick to zero in on the anatomical differences as soon as they have an opportunity to do so. Boys need to know about the anatomy of girls and vice versa.

It's important that you point out to boys and girls that each has special equipment. The common fantasy in youngsters of either sex is that everybody started off just the same but that girls had something terrible happen to them. Consequently you'll want to talk about sexual anatomy in terms of what girls *do* have rather than what they *don't* have. Once you make the facts clear, neither sex has to worry that she has been (or he might be) the victim of a gruesome fate.

The girl who asks why she doesn't have a penis needs to be told, "Honey, boys have penises; girls have vaginas." If she asks, "What's that?" tell her a vagina is an opening between her legs. If she wants to know what it's for, then you'd discuss the role of a vagina in childbirth (see Question 3).

Your child will probably ask about sexual anatomy in stages, wanting to know about the different parts at different times. As it becomes appropriate, you'll eventually want your youngster to know about the other parts of female genital anatomy: the vulva, clitoris, and urethra.

A vulva is the name given to the area between a girl's legs. This area contains the clitoris, urethra, and vagina. The clitoris is like a small "button" at the top of the vulva and is very sensitive to touch.

The urethra, vagina, and anus are the three openings between a girl's legs. The urethra is an opening for urinating. The vagina is the place a baby comes out of a mother's body when it is born. This opening is actually the end of a tube that leads to a special place inside her body called a uterus, where babies grow before they're ready to be born. The anus is the opening for bowel movements.

In addition to the penis, male genital anatomy includes the scrotum and testicles. The scrotum is like a sack that contains the testicles, sometimes called balls because they are round in shape. Like girls, boys also have an anus that allows bowel movements to leave the body.

A boy will notice that he gets erections and that they feel good. Acknowledge this matter-of-factly; "Bobby, sometimes a boy's penis gets hard, especially when it is touched. That's perfectly normal." The matter of the penis becoming part of the fathering process will usually not be asked about, nor will it need to be explained, until your child is ready to learn about sexual intercourse (typically in the elementary school years).

Boys naturally begin to compare their bodies with those of adult males. Simple statements like "Your penis will be bigger like Daddy's when you are a teenager" lets your little boy know he's perfectly normal and will grow up to become an adult male.

Eventually your boy will notice that penises come in two basic varieties, uncircumcised and circumcised. Your explanation about the presence or absence of a foreskin needs to include the basic fact that either one is normal. It's just that some parents choose to leave the piece of skin on and some don't. If it's not there, the parents have asked the doctor or rabbi to remove it just after the little boy was born.

If a boy notices he has a much smaller penis than his peers, go ahead and talk about it. Reassure him that penises, just like people, come in all sizes. All work equally well, and most of them end up being about the same size when they're erect.

The child who wants to know whether it's better to have a penis or a vagina needs to be told that neither one is better than the other, just different. If a person has a penis, that person is a boy; if a person has a vagina, that person is a girl. A person is born either a boy or a girl; when they grow up, boys can become fathers and girls can become mothers.

Sometimes girls are envious of boys' having penises because boys can urinate standing up. After all, a penis is an advantage on a camping trip or in any other place where no toilet is available! "Honey, it's true that it's easier to go to the bathroom if you have a penis. But girls can have babies and men can't, so there are advantages to having a vagina too!"

Young children will also ask questions about pubic hair and breasts. When they notice pubic hair, they may be concerned that they don't have any. A simple statement that both boys and girls grow this hair around the time they become teenagers is all that is necessary.

When your child asks about breasts, explain that girls grow breasts when they get older, sometimes by age ten or eleven. If a woman becomes a mother, her breasts become filled with milk so that she can easily feed her baby. Although breasts come in all sizes and shapes, they all work equally well.

2. WHAT DOES *MASTURBATE* MEAN?
Is it wrong to touch yourself down there?
Why does my penis get hard when I touch it?
Do girls play with themselves?

You're having a great time watching your one-year-old son playing in the bathtub. As you see him splashing in the water, you suddenly notice he's joyfully discovered a new toy. And guess what? It's attached to him!

All normal, healthy children of both sexes will discover they have genitals and that touching them feels good. This usually occurs by the first birthday.

These pleasurable feelings are not the same as the genital sexuality your child will experience after puberty. But babies do get in touch with their sensuality, and what they learn about this self-pleasuring capacity depends heavily on how the significant grown-ups in their lives react to their innocent explorations.

You probably know intellectually that all those superstitions about masturbation are false. Masturbation doesn't make you insane, nor does it cause hair to grow on your palms! While you might have religious reasons for prohibiting it, know that the urge for your child to produce these pleasurable sensations is totally normal from a physical and psychological standpoint.

Creating guilt about masturbation is often the beginning of a child's learning to think of sexual anatomy and sexual feelings as being dirty or shameful. Even though you might agree you want your child to have a healthy view of masturbation, you might still feel squeamish about talking directly to him about it.

If he asks what *masturbation* means, you might say something like "It means touching your private parts (penis, vulva). Haven't you noticed that when you touch yourself down there, you get some nice feelings?" With an older child you might want to add, "These are feelings that help prepare you to make love with someone when you're older."

Be sure to explain that this form of touching is natural: "You know, Chuck, when I was a little boy, I used to worry that it wasn't okay to masturbate, I guess because my dad never talked to me honestly about it. I just want you to know that all boys do it, so you won't have to worry about it like I did."

For the boy who wants to know why his penis becomes hard when he masturbates, explain that when he touches his penis, blood flows into it and causes it to become hard. It's called an erection, and it feels good.

For a girl asking about masturbation, you might say, "Heather, when girls touch themselves gently between their legs they get some really special feelings. Those are normal body feelings. I just want you to know that it's okay, that many girls and boys like to touch themselves there sometimes, just so you won't worry about it." Again, if she's older and understands what "making love" means, you might tell her that the feelings she gets while masturbating are similar to those she'll have when she's grown up and makes love with a man.

You do want your youngster to know, however, that masturbation is not something to be done in public. It's private business. In other words it's not to become a social experience or a spectator sport!

Masturbation is one of those subjects you'll want to bring up directly if your child doesn't ask about it during the preschool years. You might say, "Honey, have you noticed (or, I see you've noticed) it feels pretty good when you touch yourself between your legs. I just wanted you to know that many girls and boys do this, so don't think it's something weird. Do you have any questions about this?"

By bringing the subject up for discussion, you'll be giving your child important permission to ask you questions not only about masturbation but about sex in general. Such openness lays the groundwork for trust and communication with your child about any topic.

3. How Do You Make a Baby?
Why is that woman's tummy so big?
How does the baby get in there?
How does the baby come out?
Doesn't it hurt to have a baby?

Kids are naturally intrigued when they realize that babies grow inside a woman's body. Not being too much bigger than a "baby" himself, the toddler or preschooler who first hears about pregnancy looks at himself and wonders how on earth he could possibly fit inside his own mother. Even more puzzling, how on earth did he get out?

Children usually find out about pregnancy by observing a pregnant woman. Quite naturally they'll ask, "Mommy, why is her tummy so big?" or, "Why's that lady so fat?" "That lady is going to have a baby, honey. She's carrying the baby inside her body, inside her belly, and that's why her belly is so big."

It's important that you not tell your child the baby is being carried in the mother's stomach. Why? Because kids know food goes into the stomach. They also might have some vague understanding that their bowel movements result from eating food. Consequently the baby-growing-in-the-tummy explanation can be terribly confusing. A young child might wonder if she's pregnant when her "tummy" feels full or might think that babies are mixed in with bowel movements.

Either use the words *belly* or *abdomen* or explain that girls have a special place inside of them called a *uterus*. "A uterus is like a little bag that can stretch to make room for a baby to grow inside. It's located in a girl's belly, near the stomach, which holds and digests her food."

Make sure your child understands that little girls can't have babies. Only big girls, such as teenagers and women, can have babies. Even though little girls do have a uterus, it won't be ready for a baby to grow inside it for a very long time.

When your child asks how the baby gets out of the mother's body, the time has arrived for a more thorough discussion about the vagina: "A vagina is like a tube inside a girl's body that is connected to her uterus. The other end of the tube is one of the openings between her legs. A baby gets born by coming out of this opening."

You'll need to point out that a vagina is like a very thick balloon. It can easily stretch so that a baby can fit through it, but then go right back into its normal shape and size after the baby is born.

"Doesn't it hurt to have a baby?" is the next logical question. As always, tell your child the truth: Having a baby can be very uncomfortable. However, when a woman is pregnant, she can learn all about how to help the baby be born so that the process is as painless as possible. By understanding how her body works, she can help the baby come out of her body more easily. If she does have pain, doctors have medicine to give the mother to help her not feel that pain and/or can teach her breathing techniques that will help her to be more comfortable.

If you need to explain a cesarean delivery, tell your child that there are two ways of having a baby. The usual way is through the vagina, but sometimes this doesn't work. Then the doctor gives the mother medicine so she doesn't feel any pain. The doctor makes a cut through the skin on her belly and then another cut into the uterus. The doctor lifts the baby out of the mother's body and then sews the cuts back up. The cuts heal, and the mother is fine in a short time.

Kids need to know of course that women do not make babies all by themselves. There must be a father too! Preschoolers will usually accept "It takes both a mother and a father to make a baby." When your child does want to know "How does the baby get in there?" it's time for you to explain sexual intercourse (see Question 5).

4. WHY DID MY MOTHER GIVE ME AWAY?
   If I'm adopted, who are my real parents?

If your child is adopted, it's best to let her know this casually and matter-of-factly at the first appropriate opportunity. This might happen when she hears you use the word *adoption* with friends or in reference to another child and she wants to know what it means. Or it might come up when you're explaining how babies are born and you let her know she came out of another woman's body. Allowing discussion about her adoption to come up naturally gives her the healthy message that she doesn't have to feel ashamed or uneasy about it.

Once she knows she's adopted and that you're not her biological parent, she'll eventually want to know why her mother gave her away. It's best to present the birth mother's decision as an act of love.

For your young child you might simply say, "Honey, your mother loved you, but she couldn't take care of you. She wanted you to be with a family who would love you and be able to take good care of you too."

To your older youngster, you might say, "Carrie, your mother must have felt she couldn't give you the kind of life she wanted you to have. For some reason she felt she couldn't take good enough care of you, and she knew it was best for you to grow up with a mommy and a daddy who would love you and be able to give you the things you need." Or, "Honey, your mother might have known that she was too immature to be a really good mother. Or maybe things were going on in her life at the time that she knew would cause problems for a little girl. So because she loved you, she made the hard decision to give you to parents who would be better able to take care of you."

Of course many adoptions today are open, with the birth mother and adoptive parents having varying degrees of contact as the child grows up. If this is the case, you would tell your child more specifically about her natural mother's circumstances, since you'd know more of the situation than would most parents who seek a traditional adoption.

When your adopted child asks about her natural parents, give her any information you have so long as it's not severely negative (birth mother was a prostitute, abandoned the child, was in prison when she was born, etc.). Upsetting information is best left until your child is mature enough to handle such facts, probably not until her teen years.

The reason you want to present only positive information is that kids typically identify with their birth parents, even a parent of the opposite sex. If you give them information that makes their birth mothers (or natural fathers) sound like bad people, they're likely to expect themselves to develop the same qualities. So it's better just to give them positive or neutral information until they're old enough to handle negative information.

If your child uses the word *real* parents when she's referring to biological parents, realize that she's not trying to offend you (unless she says it in anger). Calmly make the distinction between *natural* parents and *real* parents: "Missy, your biological mother gave birth to you. But after that we became your 'real' parents. 'Real' parents are the people who love you and care for you while you're growing up. It's the emotional bond between us that makes us your 'real' parents even though we're not your biological parents."

Although it might raise your anxiety, let your child know that you'll be supportive of her finding out about, even contacting, her biological parents after she's an adult if she wishes. It's natural and typical for most adopted youngsters to want to find their biological parents, and this desire in no way indicates that they're rejecting you as a parent. As is the case with a natural child, their love for you will be based on your relationship with them. Finding their biological parents will not change the bond that already exists.

5. WHAT DOES *HAVING SEX* MEAN?
   What is intercourse?
   Does it hurt when you have sex?

When a young child asks you what *having sex* means, a good, easy response is: "*Having sex* means 'making love,'" or, "That's when a man and a woman make love to each other." For the older child you'll need to explain sexual intercourse.

Even if you feel comfortable talking about sexual anatomy and childbirth with your youngster, the thought of explaining sexual intercourse might fill you with anxiety. You might be tempted to put this conversation off a little longer by telling yourself, "She's just not ready." What this statement may really mean is that *you* don't feel ready to answer the question!

As with any other question, it's best answered when your child first indicates that he wants to know more about this making-love business. This could happen anytime after your child is about five. Interestingly if you show youngsters a drawing from a sex-education book depicting sexual intercourse, some five-year-olds will begin to ask questions, while many eight-or nine-year-olds will just ignore the obvious and ask nothing. In fact you might have to point out to the older child what is really going on in the drawing just to make sure he understands what intercourse is all about.

A full explanation of sexual intercourse might go something like this: "When a mother and a father make love, they lie next to each other, very close, kissing and hugging. The father's penis gets very hard and he puts it into the mother's vagina. This feels very nice to both of them, and it is a special way to show each other how much they love each other.

"A liquid called semen comes out of the father's penis into the mother's vagina. If the time is right, the mother will have a little egg, so tiny you couldn't even see it, inside of her uterus. If the liquid from the father's penis meets with that little egg, a baby will start to grow in her uterus."

If your child wants to know more about conception, tell her that a man's semen contains millions of microscopic cells called sperm, which try to penetrate the woman's egg. When one sperm succeeds, fertilization occurs, and a baby begins to grow inside the woman's uterus.

Children often wonder whether sexual intercourse hurts the woman. Again, help your youngster understand that a vagina is made up of a very elastic muscle tissue. While losing one's virginity might be uncomfortable and might even create slight bleeding, necessitating patience and gentleness on the male's part, sex should not be at all painful or uncomfortable after that first time. Explain that the woman's body secretes a special fluid in the vagina that helps make intercourse easy and pleasurable.

If a youngster happens to hear his parents making love, he may interpret the sexual sounds as evidence that someone's getting hurt. Or he might even witness sexual activity when his parents think he's asleep and are unaware that he's watching them. A child who watches sexual activity often mistakes passion for aggression.

Emphasize that sexual intercourse is a loving, delightful experience between a man and woman who love each other deeply, not something that's painful. Unfortunately most of the books explaining intercourse do so only in the context of "making babies," totally ignoring the fact that adults engage in sex far more often to share a special kind of love rather than specifically for reproduction.

Let your child know that adults have sexual intercourse even when they are not wanting to make a baby and that there are ways, called birth control, to make sure they don't make a baby unless they really want one. If your child asks for more information about birth control, tell him that there are lots of methods, many of which work by preventing the male's sperm from coming into contact with the female's egg. If he presses you further, tell him about condoms as one example of a birth-control device (see Question 10).

If you have religious beliefs that prohibit any kind of contraception, you would explain your views about this. However, you would still want your child to know that there are ways to prevent pregnancy.

Children might also ask you about other kinds of sexual activities. The best way to respond is to give a brief description of what's involved. For example, if your child's question is about oral sex, you might say, "That's when a woman kisses a man's penis" or, "That's when a man kisses a woman's vulva." Sticking to the facts in a nonjudgmental, matter-of-fact manner encourages your youngster to feel comfortable asking you questions about aspects of sexuality without belaboring the issue.

When children hear about sexual activities, it's not unusual for them to respond with shock or even horror. Comments like "Yuck!" or "That's gross!" might be their first reaction. To encourage your child to feel positive about sexuality, you might say something like "Well, honey, I understand how you feel. I used to think the same thing when I first heard about it. But as you grow up, you'll probably feel quite different." This statement acknowledges your child's fears while at the same time making it clear that you think having sex is positive and enjoyable.

6. WHY CAN'T WE PLAY WITH OUR CLOTHES OFF?
Why can't I show Johnny my bottom?

It's perfectly natural for youngsters to be curious about their bodies, especially those parts that are usually covered up. Touching these parts is also fun.

Sex play, from a child's point of view, is a fun way to spend time with a friend as well as a way to satisfy normal curiosity. The fact that kids sense that this play is a secret activity to keep hidden from grown-ups can make it all the more exciting. Consequently most youngsters will get involved in some sort of sex play with other children at one time or another.

They will play "doctor" in order to examine one another's bottoms. They might also imitate grown-up sexual activities by kissing or lying on top of each other.

You might react to finding out that your child is engaging in sex play by becoming enraged or embarrassed. In your attempt to prohibit this behavior, it's easy for you to come on too strong. It's not that you're trying to program your youngster to feel guilty about sex. It's just that you know such play can be emotionally harmful due to your child's lack of maturity and the potential for confusion, anxiety, and exploitation. It's also just plain disconcerting to find your child involved in these activities!

In order to avoid overreacting or causing your child to feel guilty about having sexual curiosities and feelings, react calmly and matter-of-factly when you find her engaged in sex play. A comment like "Okay, let's get your clothes on and come out to the kitchen for a snack," or, "I want you to keep your clothes on when you play after this. Come on out in the family room, and we'll find a video for you to watch" dilutes the intensity of the moment and gets the children ready for a different activity.

Later, when you're alone with your child, you'll want to create an opportunity to talk with him and give him the clear message that sex play is inappropriate. Try saying something like "You know, Marty, all little boys and girls are curious about what people look like naked and about how it feels to touch and be touched in private places. But I don't want you touching anyone's private parts with any part of your body—or letting them touch yours—until you're grown up. That kind of touching is only for grown-ups who love each other very much, but it's not for kids. When you get older, you'll understand more about why it's not for children."

Let your child know that if other adults, such as a friend's mother or father, find him participating in sex play, they're likely not to invite him over to play anymore. Your youngster needs to understand this is something all grown-ups feel very strongly about, and it's important for him to ask questions about sex rather than experiment with it.

Tell your child he can satisfy his curiosity about sexual matters by talking to you or to some other responsible adult: "Just ask me any questions you have about sex, Melissa, and I'll be glad to tell you the answers. We can also go to the library and find a book that will help explain these things to you. Okay?"

It's wise to contact a parent of any child who's been involved in sex play with your youngster and tell them what you observed. Most parents appreciate this courtesy and prefer to talk with their own children about sex play rather than have someone else do it for them. If you present the matter calmly and without implying blame on either child, you'll probably get a positive response from the other parent.

7. WHAT'S AN ORGASM?
   What does an orgasm feel like?

It's not at all unusual these days for young children to hear the word *orgasm* and want to know what it means. If your child is very young, don't make your answer complicated. Simply tell her, "It's a very nice feeling that people get when they make love."

If your child is older, tell him, "An orgasm is a wonderful sensation that happens when a person is being sexual, either masturbating or making love. It's the peak, or the high point and release, of sexual feelings in the body and leaves a person feeling relaxed and happy."

8. Do I Have to Have a Period?
Do periods hurt?
Isn't it gross to bleed like that?

"Periods" become a hot topic of conversation for many girls around the age of nine or so, particularly since it's not uncommon for some girls to begin menstruating as early as the fourth grade. Boys quickly pick up on the fact that something "secret" is going on with the girls (if they haven't already figured it out).

Of course many girls and boys have noticed evidence of their mother's or older sister's menstruation. Or they've found out about it because of ads for tampons and sanitary pads parading across their television screens.

A young child who asks what a tampon is can be told, "It's a piece of cotton." If she asks what the tampon is for, you might tell her, "It's something women use when they have a period." If the "What's a period?" question comes up, tell him, "It's when a woman has some bleeding from her vagina. It happens a few days every month, and it doesn't hurt."

Explaining that the period doesn't hurt is important, since kids associate blood with cuts and injuries. Tell your child directly that *this* kind of bleeding is perfectly normal and doesn't mean that something's wrong.

For an older child a more thorough explanation might be: "Menstruation is part of the process that allows women to have babies. Once a month the uterus builds up a lining as it prepares to receive a fertilized egg. If the woman doesn't become pregnant, there will be no baby and the lining is no longer needed. The uterus then sheds this lining, which is the blood that flows out of the woman's vagina when she has a period. This whole process happens about once a month from the time a girl's body is ready to make babies (ranging from about age nine to age sixteen) until her body is too old to make babies (somewhere between forty and fifty-five)."

No matter how reassuring your explanation, your child might ask, "Do I have to have a period?" or make some other remark that expresses her anxiety and/or dismay about this process ("That's gross!"). Find out what her fears are by asking directly rather than by guessing.

She might be worried that having a period will hurt if she's heard other girls or women talking about having cramps, "the curse," or feeling bad when they menstruate. Or she might know about tampons and be frightened about actually using one. She might agonize over hygiene issues or fear public embarrassment by having bloodstains on her clothes. Or she might be concerned that she'll have to give up some favorite activity, such as swimming.

Sometimes a girl's reluctance to have periods reflects her basic anxieties about growing up. She might view adulthood as difficult or dreary and want to remain a child as long as she can.

Once you know your youngster's specific concern, address it directly and give the necessary information and reassurance. If you're a woman, tell her what you worried about when you first menstruated and how you handled the situation. Even if you think your child's fears are silly, they're all too real to her. Take her concerns seriously rather than dismissing them. "Julie, I know you're not looking forward to getting your period. You haven't had one yet, so there's no way you can know what it's like until you actually experience it. Like any other change in your life, it can be both scary and exciting. Don't worry about it, you'll handle it just fine. And I'll be here to help if you need me."

Some girls become preoccupied with wondering just when they'll get their first period. A good rule of thumb is that menses begin about two years after a girl develops "breast buds." Reassure her that anytime from ages nine to sixteen is "normal" for a girl to begin menstruating so that she won't worry that she's abnormal for being on the early or the late end of the spectrum.

If your child is worrying about periods being painful, let her know that she might experience some discomfort, which can usually be relieved with an over-the-counter medication. Actual pain is not normal and should be addressed by a physician.

Above all make sure your child understands that menstruation is not an illness or a malady. It's a normal, healthy part of being a female.

9. WHAT DOES IT MEAN WHEN SOMEBODY'S GAY?
   Why are people gay?
   Is there something wrong with gay people?
   How will I know if I'm gay or not?

Most kids in elementary school quickly figure out that the word *gay* has more than one meaning. When your child asks for clarification, tell him, "A person who's gay is someone who has sex with (makes love to) another person of the same sex. Like if two men have sex with each other, or two women."

Explaining to your child *why* people are gay is much more complicated, since nobody really knows the complete answer. Current thinking is that either of two factors might be involved. The first is a hormonal difference thought to exist since birth; these men and women typically feel throughout their lives that they were born the "wrong" sex, or simply never find themselves attracted to the opposite sex.

The second factor involves early sexual experiences in which there is strong and/or repeated sexual arousal by a same-sex partner. The idea is that most of us had our sexual awakening with someone of the opposite sex and we continue that orientation, but if our early sexual arousal occurred in response to a same-sex person, we might continue a homosexual orientation.

One fact the experts are clear about is that there is no parenting pattern that explains homosexuality. Gay people, like heterosexual people, have all kinds and types of mothers and fathers.

Let your child know that being gay doesn't mean that a person is crazy or sick. Nor does it mean that the person necessarily looks or acts like someone of the opposite sex. All being gay tells you about someone is that the person has a certain sexual orientation.

Be sure your youngster knows that a homosexual experience in and of itself does not necessarily mean that a person is gay. Many heterosexual men and women have had a homosexual experience at some point in their lives, often as a teenager. Youngsters often have same-sex attractions. Helping your child know that these feelings can be just a part of growing up for some youngsters might alleviate much unnecessary anxiety about this sensitive issue.

If your child asks how a person knows whether she's gay or not, tell her that most people get a firm idea about their sexual orientation by their late teens, if they're not sure before that. Reassure her that close, affectionate feelings for someone of the same sex are not indications of homosexuality and are quite different from the specific feelings of repeated sexual arousal that occur in people who become gay: "Lisa, just because you and Sally like to give each other hugs certainly doesn't mean that either one of you is gay!"

10. WHAT IS "SAFE SEX"?
    What is AIDS?
    How do people get AIDS?
    What's a condom?

When the matter of "safe sex" comes up, be grateful. After all, this gives you an opportunity to let your child know about unsafe sex!

Not that you'll want to go into a complicated explanation about techniques of birth control or gory descriptions of sexually transmitted diseases. This would be inappropriate for most children in elementary school. But you can tell your youngster that there is such a thing as birth control and that there are diseases that people can catch when they have sex. You might say something like "Jeremy, 'safe sex' means making sure you don't create a baby when you don't want one and making sure you don't catch any diseases from having sex."

AIDS, of course, is the disease your child is most likely to hear about. Explain that AIDS is a very serious disease that people can catch from having sex or from using an infected needle (when they shoot drugs into their veins or have a blood transfusion). A pregnant woman with AIDS can also pass the disease to her unborn child, who is then born with it. People are talking a lot about this disease because there's no cure for it yet, and people die from it. Doctors want us to know we mustn't stick needles in our arms or have sex with anyone without knowing specifically how to protect ourselves from this disease.

If your child asks how a person can keep from making a baby when she has sex or how to keep from getting a sexual disease, explain about condoms. "A condom is like a balloon that fits over the man's penis. It keeps the woman from getting pregnant and it also helps to ensure that neither person gets any diseases from having sex."

11. WHEN CAN I HAVE SEX?
How old do you have to be to have sex?
Do I have to be married before I have sex?

If a young child asks you when he can have sex, say something like "When you're grown up" or, "When you get married." This is likely to be all the explanation he'll want. "Sex is for grown-ups, honey" is another good answer.

The older elementary school child is likely to recognize that many people have sex before they're married and that many teens, who don't qualify as grown-ups, also become sexually active. They might well challenge your statements about waiting to be an adult or waiting to be married. So what do you say?

Save your recommendations about the criteria a person should meet before becoming sexually active for when your youngster is a teenager. At this point simply acknowledge that many people do not abide by the standards you've just stated (adulthood, marriage) but that you still feel your answer is best: "The decision about when to begin having sex is very important, Stephanie. Many kids take this too lightly and get themselves into trouble. Before you begin dating, we'll sit down and talk about this more so that you'll have all the information you need before you make your own decision."

MORE SUGGESTIONS

1. Don't be afraid to teach your child the correct names for parts of the sexual anatomy. Although there's nothing wrong with using the family's pet slang, it's helpful to introduce kids to the "real" terms as well.

2. There are many good sex-education books written just for children. Pick one that's appropriate for your youngster to read or, if she's younger, for you to read with her. Seeing the illustrations and hearing or reading the words in the book allows your child to clear up any confusion. Using a book also helps you break the ice if you feel uncomfortable or anxious talking with your child about sexual matters.

3. Use talking about sexual anatomy as an opportunity to teach your child how to protect herself from child molestation. Explain that sexual parts of the body are "private parts" not to be looked at "up close" or touched by anyone except when visiting a doctor in his office or when a parent needs to check out a child's bottom to see if medicine is needed. "Honey, if anyone ever tries to get you to take your underwear off for them or tries to touch you in a way that makes you uncomfortable, be sure to tell me about it."

4
Divorce/Remarriage

"I FEEL LIKE A TOSSED SALAD" IS A STATEMENT RECENTLY MADE BY A TEN-year-old whose parents had been divorced about three months. Unfortunately his words sum up one of the most typical problems faced by kids whose parents divorce: being emotionally caught in the middle between two warring parents who both sincerely believe they have their child's best interest at heart.

Whether you or your partner initiated the divorce, you probably agonized about the effects on your child of ending your marriage. The split might not have been so difficult if abuse or intense fighting was the issue; if such were the case, you probably felt that your children would be better off not having to cope with such a negative situation.

If you're like many parents, however, your marriage ended not because either you or your mate was a "bad guy" or because the children were being exposed to some dangerous situation, but because your relationship with your mate had become emotionally dead. You might have grown apart or were mismatched from the beginning. If you weren't modeling a vital, warm, affectionate marital relationship, you might have concluded there was no benefit being in an unsatisfactory marriage "for the sake of the children."

Kids frequently have significant adjustment problems in the months after their parents separate or divorce. Their grades might drop, they might become very sad and/or angry, they might have behavior problems at home or in school, and they might regress to more immature behavior (bed-wetting, baby talk, fear of being alone in a room, tantrums, psychosomatic ailments, etc.).

Children almost always want their parents to remain together no matter what the circumstances. It's perfectly normal for them to fantasize that their parents will reunite one day, even after one or both parents remarry. Living in a one-parent home or a blended family simply isn't the same as living with your own two parents.

Despite all these obstacles, kids with divorced parents do adjust, many of them quite well. The major influence on the child's adjustment is the emotional state of the parent with whom the child lives. If this parent maintains a positive attitude and is emotionally stable, the child is likely to fare well. A second factor is the reliability of the noncustodial parent in maintaining predictable contact with the child. Less frequent visits that occur regularly are better for the child than the situation where the child never knows when (or if) he will or won't see the other parent.

Another key factor in a youngster's adjustment to divorce is the degree to which her parents cooperate with each other and, even more important, the degree to which those parents stay out of the destructive interactions that cause a child to feel loyalty conflicts. Parents who handle their divorce in a positive, mature way truly put the needs of their children ahead of their own personal preferences. When this happens, a child's initial adjustment difficulties typically resolve within the first year after the separation. If parents cannot maintain a nonhostile, mutually supportive role, their children's initial problems might become compounded and result in serious emotional consequences.

1. WHY ARE YOU AND DADDY GETTING A DIVORCE?
   How come you and Mommy don't love each other anymore?
   Did you get divorced because of me?

You might find these questions hard to answer for a number of reasons. You probably have mixed feelings yourself about getting a divorce and might worry about becoming emotional when you talk about it. If you feel you are being forced into a divorce, it's especially difficult to talk to your child about the reasons.

Also, you know your youngster is going to be upset by the news, even if she doesn't show it at first. Your natural protective instincts make you wish you could shield her from any kind of bad news or emotional upset. Because you want to traumatize her as little as possible, you're anxious about the way you present the subject and want to do it "right."

It's usually best for you and your mate to tell your child about your separation or divorce when both of you are present. If you have more than one child, telling all the children together is preferable, as it promotes a sense of closeness between siblings.

The simplest beginning is direct and honest: "Honey, we have some sad news. Your mother and I have decided that we are not going to be married anymore" or, "Your dad is going to move into an apartment. We're going to live apart for a while to decide if we still want to be married to each other." Or, "As you know, Melinda, your mom and I haven't been getting along very well for a long time. We've decided to get a divorce. I'll be moving into an apartment this weekend."

Address the "why?" by stating the truth without going into gory details. Youngsters do need you to give them a reason to help them understand what's going on, but they don't need you to attack your partner's character or reveal highly personal information that you would normally not disclose to your child.

The following are all succinct but honest ways of clarifying the situation for your child: "Maggie, you know, your dad and I have been having lots of arguments about his drinking." "Mom and I hardly ever agree about money, and we end up being mad at each other most of the time." "Your dad and I still care a great deal for each other, but we realize we like very different things now. You dad likes to do things alone, and I'm really a people person." "Sometimes people who live together a long time simply change and have different goals. Your dad wants me to stay home most of the time, but I really want to have a career."

If your marriage is ending because of infidelity, what you do or don't tell your child about this depends on the circumstances and the likelihood of the child's knowing (or learning about) it. If, sadly, one parent's unfaithfulness has been blatant and your child knows or asks about it, calmly explain the situation: "Jeremy, your mother has been spending time with Frank for some time now and this has been something we disagree about." Or, for a younger child, "I don't like Mommy spending so much time with Frank."

If your child seems totally unaware that infidelity is an issue, there's no more reason to bring this up than any other aspect of your sexual relationship. But if your marriage is breaking up because one partner is committed to a third party, it's probably better to tell your child up front that your mate has decided he wants to be with the other person. Kids are not stupid and will quickly figure out the truth when this new person is around a parent all the time.

Although some adults divorce by mutual agreement, most of the time it's only one parent who wants to end the marriage. Trying to pull off a fake togetherness and pretend that both parties are in agreement about this only builds mistrust in your child. Since the truth will soon become evident, go ahead and matter-of-factly tell your youngster, "Honey, I really don't want a divorce but your dad thinks it's best."

Whatever your reasons for the divorce, let your child understand that your decision was well thought out and not something you decided easily or impulsively: "I've been thinking about this for over a year, Josh. It's a very hard decision to make, and I'm very sad that your dad and I couldn't work things out."

When your child asks why you and your spouse don't love each other anymore, realize she will understandably have trouble grasping the point that one parent can still love the other one but not want to stay married. Explain: "There are many different kinds of love. I love your mom in the sense that I care about her and don't want anything bad to happen to her. But there's a special kind of loving feeling a man and woman are supposed to have for one another, and I just don't feel that way anymore about your mom. I know it's very hard to understand right now, but hopefully you'll understand it better as you get older."

Know that most children will ask themselves at some point, "Did I cause my parents to get a divorce?" Even if there have been no arguments specifically about them, they'll still wonder about it. Remember that young children blame themselves for anything negative that happens in the family. It's easier to think they caused the problem than to realize their parents aren't omnipotent and perfect.

Reassure your youngster that the divorce has nothing to do with her: "Stacy, your dad and I want you to know that you had nothing to do with our getting a divorce. We've had problems getting along since long before you were even born." Or, "Your mom and I have had problems for many years, which have nothing at all to do with you."

Just as you make it clear that your child has no blame in the marital difficulties, let him know that he doesn't have any power to fix the situation either. Kids sometimes think they'll get their parents back together if they behave extremely well or extremely badly.

If you think this might be happening, you could introduce this topic by asking, "Some kids wonder if they might be able to do something to get their parents back together. Have you ever thought about that, honey?" If he has, tell him, "You know, Sammy, you could be the best boy in the world, make all A's, and clean your hamster cage every night; it's still not going to bring your dad and me back together. We are the only ones who can decide about staying together or splitting up." Or, "Honey, you could make all F's, get into fights every day at school, and be the worst kid on the block. Your mom and I would be very upset about this, but we still wouldn't decide to stay married. We'd just have to find ways to help you with those problems."

Make sure your child understands that both of you are still going to be his parents even though you two aren't living together. Each of you loves him; each of you will always be there for him. Give him permission to come to either one of you with any question, feeling, or thought he might have. Tell him that even if he thinks you'll be upset with something he might say or ask, it's okay; you want him to confide in both of you.

2. WHOSE FAULT IS IT?
Is Mommy bad?
Should I be mad at Daddy too?

Difficult as it might be, don't put blame for the divorce either on yourself or on the other parent. It really does take two to make a relationship work and two to mess it up. It's best to teach your child this fact, even if one of you *seems* to be the obvious one to blame.

Placing blame just makes kids feel that they have to take sides. You might say something like "Tammy, your dad and I both created the problems we've had in our marriage. Neither of us meant to, but it happened. It's a very sad thing for all of us."

While you might not directly blame your spouse in so many words, be aware that character assassination is just another way of trying to get your child to see all the marital problems as the other parent's fault. If you need to make negative statements in order to be truthful, stick with a factual explanation without adding judgments or calling names.

With a younger child keep your explanations general: "Your mom has difficulty controlling her temper," or, "We just didn't agree about how to spend money," or, "Your dad and I have different ideas about how we like to spend our time." Your older child could be told more specifically about issues such as a parent's having a drinking problem, being addicted to pills, or having serious emotional problems.

Of course when you are emotionally bruised from a divorce (or from the litigation to obtain it), it's awfully tempting to lean on your youngster for emotional support. If you turn your child into your confidant, however, you blur the parent-child boundaries that are so important to maintain. Your confiding in your child actually becomes a burden to her. She then has to worry about taking care of your emotions, and to do that, she might feel that she must take your side against the other parent. Particularly if your child lives with you, she'll feel pressured to take your side so that you won't be angry with her. You are her sole caretaker now, and as such you are a very powerful figure in her life.

Another reason you don't want to place your child in a position of being your "best friend" is that he might feel he has to take the place of the other parent. Better to have your own adult friends than to force your youngster into a role where he's taking care of you rather than the other way around.

Your youngster might also ask if one parent is "bad" or might begin to denounce the other parent as "bad" or "wrong." If this happens, you might say something like "Honey, I didn't like that behavior, either, but your mom has many fine qualities, and we all make mistakes." Why protect the other parent? Because kids need to feel there are positive aspects of each parent in order to feel really good about themselves. If they see one parent as a terrible person for whatever reason, they're likely to believe unconsciously that some part of them is also terrible since they are in fact that parent's child.

Also, think about how you feel if someone criticizes your parents or close family members. Chances are you become very defensive, even if you inwardly agree with the person's viewpoint. You probably feel irritated with the person doing the criticizing as well and are unlikely to be very receptive to any further conversation at that moment. Kids have these same kinds of feelings when a parent is criticized, even if the content of the information is correct.

If your child asks if she should be mad at her other parent, you might be tempted to try to develop an emotional ally. But if you deliberately try to get your youngster to side with you against your ex, know that your strategy is likely to backfire when he gets older. Many young adults become very embittered toward a parent who they realized kept them away from or turned them against the other parent.

3. WHY CAN'T I PICK WHO I WANT TO LIVE WITH?
Won't Mommy be lonely if I don't live with her?
Will Dad still love me if I live with you?

It's important that children not be put in the position of choosing which parent they want to live with. Child-custody battles become extremely destructive when youngsters are pushed into voicing a preference or, more often, forced to answer questions that put one parent in a bad light. The resulting guilt can be long-lasting and very damaging emotionally.

Even if a youngster has a preference, she shouldn't be forced into stating it. Most kids in that situation will tell you that they don't want to decide which parent they'll live with; the burden is just too great. Besides, the real truth is that most children really want to live with both parents!

Interestingly it isn't uncommon for parents to come to a mental-health professional who is performing a custody evaluation with each parent genuinely believing he or she is the child's preferred parent. Each will honestly report statements by the child that "prove" the child wants to live with him or her. The truth is, children have a difficult time not telling a parent what he or she wants to hear. Is it any wonder a youngster will tell both parents she wants to live with them?

To take this burden off your child, tell him that you and the other parent will decide together where he will live and that you'll both make that decision knowing he really would like to live with each of you. If you and your ex can't agree, tell him that a judge will make this important decision based on information he receives from each parent. The judge will make a decision based on what is in the child's best interest, even though the judge knows that *each* parent wants to live with the child. When a decision is made, acknowledge your child's normal sadness about missing one parent while living with or visiting the other.

Sometimes your youngster will worry that the parent he's not living with will be lonely without him. Reassure him the other parent certainly will miss him when he's not around, but that the parent is a grown-up who is responsible for making her own life happy: "Honey, I know Mom misses you a lot, but she has her job and friends to keep her busy and to have fun with while she's looking forward to seeing you. You two can talk on the phone anytime, and of course you'll be visiting her regularly."

But what if the other parent isn't doing well emotionally and your child knows she's very depressed? The message you want to get across is that while you feel sorry this is happening to your ex, it's not the child's responsibility or yours: "Sammy, I know Mom is having a tough time right now. But none of us can make another person happy. Your mom's got to figure out how to get herself feeling better, maybe with the help of a counselor. All you can do is let her know you love her and want her to find some way to be happier with her life."

If your child asks if the other parent will still love her if she lives with you, reassure her that a parent's love doesn't stop when a child moves away. Let her know the other parent still loves her even when she's with you and vice versa. Encourage her to keep in touch with the other parent by phone or letters. The best thing for your child is to feel permission to be close to both of you.

4. WHY DOESN'T DADDY COME TO SEE ME?
   If Mommy loves me, why did she leave?

What if you're in the position of having an ex-mate who, for whatever reason, doesn't keep in contact with your child or does so only sporadically and unpredictably? Perhaps the other parent doesn't exercise visitation privileges consistently or at all. Or he may not keep in touch by phone or letter, possibly even ignoring important events, such as the child's birthday or religious holidays.

There's a fine line between giving the other parent the benefit of the doubt and actually lying to cover for him or her. Without disorting the truth, you'll want to try to explain the other parent's behavior in a manner that's least likely to cause your child to feel unloved.

For a young child you might make statements like "Terry, your dad loves you very much. I don't know why he promises to visit you and then doesn't show up sometimes. I know he wouldn't do it if he could help it. I just don't know the reason." Or, "Honey, your dad was never one to give presents for birthdays. Some people are just like that, but it doesn't mean he doesn't love you." Be sure to ask your child what she's feeling, acknowledging any hurt or anger that surfaces.

As your child gets older, you'll need to give her more information or admit frankly that you don't know the answer. The longer the situation continues, the more difficult it may be for you to remain positive without becoming deceitful. The way to steer a middle course might be to be compassionately matter-of-fact about what's happening and open about the confusing array of feelings that result: "I'm sorry your dad doesn't keep in touch with you more, Jason; I know it hurts your feelings. I really don't know why your dad is like that, and I'm angry with him too." Or, "Honey, your mom has never been very reliable about coming to see you. When I last saw her, she was very troubled and had lots of personal problems, which have nothing to do with you. Sometimes people love their kids, but they just don't know how to be very good parents because they are so troubled themselves."

Encourage your child to express her feelings about the other parent's behavior. Remember to ask open-ended questions so that you don't get caught in the trap of putting words in her mouth. Once you know what she's feeling, you can make reassuring comments such as "I'm sorry you're disappointed you didn't hear from your dad today, honey. And I understand how you're kind of mad when he tells you he'll come see you and doesn't show up without any explanation."

A very difficult concept to get across is the fact that a youngster is not unlovable even if a parent is unable to show love for him. The deficiency is in the parent, not the child. "Your dad loves you as much as he can love anybody, but he has problems showing his love. You're a wonderful boy any dad would be proud of, honey. It's your dad's problem and it has nothing to do with you."

If your child communicates at all with the other parent, encourage her to be assertive about wanting more contact and to discuss it directly with your ex. That also means telling that parent her feelings of anger, sadness, and hurt. Role-play the situation with her to help her handle this appropriately and to build her confidence. With an older youngster you might encourage her to write the other parent a letter explaining her feelings.

If your youngster was abandoned by the other parent, she might ask how the parent who left could do so if that parent loved her. Let her know that that parent was just too troubled to be a responsible parent. To make sure she doesn't blame herself, stress that the problem lay within the parent. Help her see that parent as having a personality deficiency or emotional problem, which prevented him from being a good parent. Tell the truth in matter-of-fact, nonjudgmental terms: "Molly, your dad had problems doing what he said he'd do," or, "Honey, Dad had a problem with drugs and it made him unable to be responsible to anybody," or simply "Your dad had many good qualities, but he just wasn't grown up enough to be a parent." You can empathize with your child's feelings without performing a character assassination on your ex.

In spite of your own feelings about the other parent, make sure you leave some hope for your child. Let her know that one day, perhaps when she's older or even an adult, she and the other parent might develop a relationship if she wants to. People do change, and many parents and youngsters repair their relationships when a child becomes an adult.

5. WHY CAN'T I GO TO CAMP ANYMORE?
   Are we going to have enough money?
   Daddy gives you child support for me. Why can't I have any of it?
   How come we have to move?
   Why do you have to work more now?

The fact is that many children's lifestyles change when their parents divorce. If the youngster lives with the parent with the lesser income, chances are she'll live in a less expensive home with a smaller budget for necessities such as clothes and with fewer opportunities for enrichment activities such as lessons, summer camp, and trips.

If you were forced into a divorce against your wishes and have a more restricted lifestyle as a result, it's hard not to discuss this situation with your child without sounding bitter toward your ex-spouse. It might help to remember, though, that one of the primary messages you want to give your child is that a person can remain positive in the face of obstacles.

It's best to answer these questions with a factual account of the situation: There used to be money for both piano lessons and gymnastics; now there is money for only one, or perhaps none. Instead of laying blame for the tight budget, focus on helping your child express his normal feelings of disappointment, anger, and frustration about there being less money to spend. "I know you were counting on going to camp this summer, honey. I'm really sorry we don't have the money for it this year," or, "Theresa, I don't blame you for feeling angry about giving up your dance lessons. I'm really sorry I can't provide them for you." With an older child, of course, you might discuss the possibility of her earning money, which could help out with costs.

If your child asks if there's going to be enough money, don't overwhelm him with the details of your finances, but be realistic and truthful with him. It's pointless to try to pretend everything's the same when it isn't. Your youngster will develop more trust in you if you explain the money situation in terms she can understand: "We're going to be fine, honey, but we're going to have to cut back on some expenses. That means I won't be going to the beauty parlor every week and I'll be cleaning the house myself. We won't be eating out quite as much, so let's sit down and make a list of some foods you'd like me to get at the grocery store. We're also going to start buying our clothes when the sales are on. Those are my ideas; now, can you think of some other ways we might be able to save some money?"

To help your child feel he's making a contribution to the family, you might assign him some additional chores or encourage him to begin saving part of his allowance to buy something he wants. By involving him in budget-cutting decisions and getting his suggestions, you help develop the feeling that your family is pulling together for the good of everyone. When he feels included in the process, he's less likely to see the world as "doing a number" on him and will feel he has some control over his world.

Remember to listen to your child's concerns whenever the family faces any stressful situation or lifestyle change. Realize that the best lesson you can give your youngster is for her to see you cope with problems rather than deny them. Your modeling how a mature adult deals with difficult situations gives her a more realistic picture of the world and better prepares her for the struggles she might face in her future.

If your youngster realizes you're getting child support, she might ask why she can't have it. After all it's for her, isn't it? Explain that you do use the child support money to pay part of her expenses, but those expenses might include things like the house payment, the car, doctor bills, school costs, clothes, and many other items you provide for her. Without it you might be living in a smaller house, have an older car, and so on. In other words help her see that child-support money provides more benefits for her than you would be able to provide without it.

If your child has to move from the house she's called home, she might ask why this needs to happen. While it's fun and easy to move from a small house to a big one, or a less expensive one to an expensive one, the reverse is difficult even for adults. If this is the case, be honest; let him know you're also struggling with the situation: "Honey, moving to this home has been hard on all of us. We all miss those things we used to take for granted. Now that we're here, though, let's figure out a way to make it really special for us. Do you have any ideas?"

Another common lifestyle change resulting from divorce is when a mother who has not been employed or who has worked part-time must take a full-time job. For a child this might mean going to day care or coming home and not having an adult around for a few hours.

If your child asks why you have to work more, let her know that your new work schedule is necessary because you have to make more money. But realize it's not just the hours you're working that could be bothering her but the change in lifestyle that happens when a parent who's been home most of the time begins to work full-time.

For instance you might begin to fix very simple meals or eat carry-out food more often. While you might have been used to watching television in the evenings, helping with homework, playing games with your youngster, reading to him, or doing other leisure-time activities, you might now find yourself spending most of your evenings doing laundry or catching up on housework.

Obviously these changes are going to affect your child. Don't exhaust yourself trying to be Superparent. Explain to your youngster that your work situation has changed, what those changes involve, and how all this affects her. Let her know you'll have less overall time to spend with her, but reassure her that you intend to make special time for her as often as possible. Ask her to help you think of some ways the two of you can spend time together. Don't think just in terms of fun things, but also include ways you and your child can work together: "Tell you what, Janie; you help me clean up Saturday mornings for a couple of hours and then we'll go get hamburgers and rent a movie. Okay?"

Realize that your child's emotional antennae will pick up on your attitudes toward your living circumstances and financial situation. If you're preoccupied with the unfairness of life and dwelling on what might have been, so will your child. Instead become a model for her of a person who uses your energy making the best of things without denying the reality of normal feelings such as sadness, fear, anger, and frustration.

6. WHY CAN'T I VISIT DADDY WHENEVER I WANT TO?
   I don't want to visit Dad. Do I have to go?
   But why can't I be with you on Christmas?

Visitation arrangements can be very confusing to children. After all, they're typically used to seeing both of their parents on a daily basis; suddenly they have to go by a schedule that makes no sense to them.

Kids are lucky when their divorced parents are able to work out an informal arrangement that is flexible both for the parents and the child. Unfortunately it's more common for youngsters to have visitation set for them by the court. Either the parents cannot agree on a mutually acceptable schedule, or they're likely to get into arguments or power plays when they have to communicate about visitation (or anything else) on an ongoing basis. While not ideal, set visitation can spare the youngster the trauma of being used as a pawn in the parents' continued animosity toward each other.

If your child asks to see the other parent outside of the visitation schedule and either you or your ex do not want her to go, tell her, "Amanda, your weekend with your dad starts the Friday after this one. But why don't you give him a call tonight?" Or, "Honey, we have to go by the court's schedule. I'm sorry it worked out that way, and I know it's hard for you to understand, but that's just the way it is."

Sometimes a child will ask to visit the other parent because she is angry at the parent she's with. She might not like a rule or some discipline she's been given, so she uses the "Why can't I go live with . . . ?" as a threat. This situation demands the utmost cooperation from parents if the youngster is not to become a master manipulator.

It's best for each parent to make it clear to the child that she's going to get angry at whomever she's living with at times; this happens in every family, even ones with two parents living under the same roof. When she's angry, she needs to learn to work things out with the parent she's mad at rather than run to the other parent. It's the parents (or the court) who will decide if some change in visitation needs to occur, not the child.

Of course sometimes the problem is that your child is supposed to visit the other parent and doesn't want to. She might protest and ask if she has to go. No matter what your sentiments on the subject, it's best to remain matter-of-fact as you say something like "I'm sorry you don't want to go this weekend, Josh, but it is your dad's weekend and he'd be very upset if you don't go," or simply "I'm sorry, Thad, but you have to go by the court's schedule."

You'll certainly want to try to find out why your child is objecting to the visitation so that you can make suggestions to correct the problem. Encourage him to tell the other parent if something is happening during the visitation that bothers him. "Honey, why don't you tell your mom how you feel about her watching so much television when you're there?" or, "Lance, I'm sure your dad would want to know you don't care for some of the food he fixes. Why don't you give him ideas about what kind of food you would like?"

Realize that if you and your ex aren't on friendly terms, your child might try to manipulate you by tattling on the other parent. Kids become geniuses at pushing their parents' emotional buttons. If they're mad at the other parent, they might give you information they think will get that parent in trouble. If they're trying to butter you up for something, they might say things they know you'll want to hear so that you'll be in a good mood and will grant their wishes.

Holidays can be particularly difficult for kids who have to split their time between their parents. Each parent generally prefers to have the youngster on those special one-day celebrations like Thanksgiving, birthdays, and religious holidays. Ideally a youngster could spend half her time with each parent, but this rarely happens unless parents are extremely flexible and cooperative. When visitation is regulated by a divorce decree, those special days are usually alternated yearly.

Sometimes kids have a definite preference to be with a particular parent on a holiday and feel anguish about being forced to spend the occasion with the other parent. Hard as it is, it's best to acknowledge his feelings but encourage him to go and have a good time: "Honey, I know you'd prefer to stay here for Christmas, and you know I'd love to have you here. But it's your mom's turn this year, and I want you to go and have fun. We'll have our own celebration when you get back." If you're obviously distraught over the situation, you only invite your youngster to feel guilty about having to leave and/or guilty about having a good time.

7. WHY DO I HAVE TO WHEN DADDY DOESN'T MAKE ME DO THAT AT HIS HOUSE!
   Mom says I'm not allowed to do that, so who should I listen to?

One of the most frustrating situations for kids and parents alike occurs when parents have different views about what kids should and shouldn't do. When the parents are married to one another, at least they have the opportunity (ideally) to voice their own views, reach a compromise, and unite on one set of guidelines on most issues. When parents are divorced, however, neither has any power over establishing the rules in the other parent's household.

While the ideal situation would be for you and your ex to establish rules jointly that are the same in both homes, this doesn't happen often. You, your ex, and your child all need to understand that there are different rules at Mom's house and Dad's house. Explain this to your child by using the analogy of his spending the night with a friend: He would need to respect the house rules no matter how they differ from the rules at his home, and he certainly wouldn't argue about them with the adult in charge.

If your youngster protests that you're asking her to do something the other parent doesn't require, simply state the facts: "Martha, your dad and I have different rules. When you're at my house, you have to live by mine. That's just the way the cookie crumbles!" or, "Honey, I know your mom doesn't give you a set bedtime, but around here you'll be in bed by eight-thirty on school nights."

If you acquiesce to your child's pressure to abide by the other parent's rules, you run the risk of being easily manipulated. Many parents have been shocked to discover that they were suckered into giving their child permission to go somewhere, participate in some activity, or buy something because their youngster told them the other parent allows it—only to learn that the other parent is furious with them for permitting such a thing!

Of course sometimes kids bring up issues not because they're trying to manipulate parents but because they're genuinely confused by their parents' differing values. Your child might ask who she should listen to when you tell her she can do something the other parent won't allow. Admit the difference and explain your reasons for your opinion: "Jake, I know your dad lets you see R-rated movies at his house, but I just don't agree with that. When you're with me, you can't rent them," or, "Honey, I think church attendance is very important but your mom has never agreed. I'm going to insist that you go to church with me when you're here on Sundays. When you're grown up, you can make your own decision about this."

Explain differences between you and your ex the same way you'd explain differences between your family and the family of your child's best friend. "They believe their way is best; I don't agree. They're free to do what they want, but in this house we'll do it this way."

8. WHY DOES DAN SLEEP HERE WHEN YOU'RE NOT MARRIED
   TO HIM?
   Does she have to spend the night with us?

People differ greatly on the subject of whether or not a single parent should sleep with a boyfriend or girlfriend when a child is around to know about it. The important thing, as is true with any other moral issue, is to tell your child what you believe is best. If your standard is different from that of your youngster's friends or the community in general, you need to relay this information to her so that she'll be prepared to deal with people's reactions.

Young children usually don't make an issue of someone sleeping over unless some adult calls it to their attention (like the other parent or the grandparents). Older children, however, are aware of the conventional stance that people shouldn't sleep together unless they're married.

If you choose to have another adult sleep with you when your child is around, you'll need to discuss the matter openly. Explain your relationship to this person and acknowledge that the two of you are sleeping together: "Maggie, you know that Don and I are very special to each other, so Don will be staying here overnight once in a while. Sometimes kids have feelings about this. Do you, honey?"

You'll ask this question because you want to give your child the opportunity to show if she has any concern about the sleeping arrangements. If she does, you'll need to address them: "Well, I know some people believe a man and woman shouldn't sleep together until they're married, but I don't really feel that way. I think there are circumstances when it's okay for people to sleep together before they're married if they have a special relationship. I'll explain more about this when you're a little older."

If your child indicates that she wants to know more, tell her what you really believe. For instance you might say, "Don and I are very much in love, Maggie, and we plan to get married if everything works out as well as we think it will," or, "I feel it's okay for a man and woman to sleep together if they care deeply about each other and are in a committed relationship."

What if your child says, "Well, Amy's mom told Amy you shouldn't sleep with someone unless you're married!" Again, point out that people have different opinions on many subjects. They are entitled to their opinions, and you are entitled to yours.

The point is if you feel comfortable with your decision, you will communicate your comfort to your child. If you are uneasy with it, your youngster will pick up on your anxiety. Kids are usually able to handle situations their parents are comfortable with even when others disagree.

But what if your child objects? Some children make it very clear that they don't like such an arrangement. It might be they're jealous of the attention you give this other person, they're afraid that your sleeping with this person means you're going to get married soon, or they're upset because they think your ex will be upset. Or maybe they simply don't like this other person.

While it's important to let your child know you value her opinions, you don't want to give her the idea you need her permission before you make your decisions. You need to establish clear boundaries about what is and what isn't in your youngster's control.

You might explain by saying something like "Annie, I know you don't like the idea of my having a girlfriend. I can understand that. But it's important for grown-ups to have relationships with other adults as well as with their children. If you have a problem with my girlfriend, I certainly want to know about it and I'll try my best to figure out a way to work things out so that we call can get along. But

Janet is my girlfriend, and she'll be staying here with us some of the time."

9. WHY SHOULD I LISTEN TO YOU? YOU'RE NOT MY DAD!
   Dad, why should I have to obey my stepmother?
   Do I have to love my stepdad?
   Is he trying to be my daddy?

When a parent remarries, a child is bound to have mixed feelings about a stepparent. Typically the child will challenge the authority of this new member of the family at some point. This might happen immediately or after a honeymoon phase, when everyone in the new blended family is on his best behavior. But it inevitably happens!

Let your child understand that when any new member enters a family, be it a stepparent, a baby, or a relative, the needs and preferences of that person must be considered too. That includes following the rules a parent and stepparent will establish. If you're the natural parent, make it clear that when you're not around, the other adult does have authority.

If you are a stepparent and a child challenges you because you're not his natural parent, let him know that you are an adult and that he must respect your wishes and feelings. "Vic, I know I'm not your dad. But I am living here, and your mother and I have agreed on certain rules. You need to listen to me just like you'd listen to any adult, with consideration and respect."

If you are the natural parent and your child wants to know why she should have to obey a stepparent, tell her, "Holly, Brad is your stepfather and you do need to listen to him and respect his feelings. I know he's not your father, but you need to treat him in the same manner you'd treat any other adult in this house. If you don't like something he asks you to do or the way he treats you, tell him or me and we'll all discuss it."

Sometimes a child will ask if she has to love a stepparent. Reassure her that you'll never force her to love anyone, but that you hope she and her stepparent can like each other. Resist the temptation to tell your child you want her and her stepparent to be "friends"; friends are on an equal basis and don't set rules for one another.

Realize that it's hard for your child to care for a stepparent without feeling disloyal to your ex, particularly if the latter invites the child to feel guilty about it. Sometimes a youngster will begin to develop a better relationship with the stepparent than the natural parent and then back away in fear of the natural parent's reaction. And sometimes a child won't allow herself to get close to a stepparent for the same reason.

Let your youngster know that just as you consider her feelings, you want her to consider yours. A stepparent is, after all, someone you've chosen to be in that role. You love this person, and you want your child to respect that fact: "I love your stepfather very much, and my wishes are important just as yours are, honey. I want you to give Mike a chance, and I hope you two will like each other."

Your child might also ask directly if a stepparent is trying to take the place of the natural parent of the same sex. Reassure him that you would never expect another adult to substitute for the natural parent and that neither you nor the stepparent wish to get in the way of his relationship with that natural parent: "Honey, Harry is not trying to take your father's place. It's just that when you are with us, you'll need to follow the rules we've set. Your father might do things quite differently, but this is our house and we make the rules here."

Allow your youngster's relationship with a stepparent to develop at the child's pace. Be patient and give it time. But in a gentle manner make it clear that the stepparent does have a say in what goes on in your house. Your child should treat him or her with the same respect he'd treat a teacher, coach, or other authority figure.

10. WHY ARE YOU ALWAYS SO NICE TO *HIS* KIDS?
When it's my weekend with you, why does she have *to be here?*
Why do you let her *kids do it when you won't let me do it?*
Why don't you make his *kids do the same thing?*

When your significant other or new mate has children, your own child is naturally going to feel some rivalry with them. He might resent the fact that you include these children in your time with him, and he'll be vigilant about noticing any behavior of yours that he thinks shows your preferential treatment of them.

If your youngster asks why you're nicer to someone else's kids than to her, she's expressing jealousy and insecurity. Rather than jumping to defend your behavior, ask her how she thinks you're being nicer to the other children. After you've listened, admit any unfairness on your part if there is any. Point out that even if you are or seem to be unfair sometimes, you still love her. Reassure her that you'll always feel a special love for her because she's your child and that your relationship with any other child will never change that. However, make it clear that you intend to be caring and friendly to any child you're with, just as you want your child to be friendly to all adults, not just to you.

If your child asks why the other parent is not spending exclusive time with her during visitation, encourage her to let your ex know she's wanting some time one-on-one. But make it clear that she's being unreasonable to expect to have her other parent totally to herself when that parent lives with other children. Whatever your own feelings about your ex's remarriage or living arrangements, be realistic about what is reasonable to expect in such circumstances.

If your youngster asks why you have to include a significant other or mate during his visitation, you might say, "Honey, I'll make sure we spend some time alone when you visit, but remember I do have Sally's children here too. We'll all need to spend some time together." Again, reassure him of his special place in your heart: "Rob, you'll always be very special to me; I love you very much. My being with Sally or her kids (or loving Tommy and Samantha) doesn't take anything away from your and my relationship."

Your child will quickly pick up on any differences in the rules or expectations you might have for him compared with those you have for the children of your significant other or new mate. If he asks why you allow someone else's kids to do something you won't allow him to do (or why you don't make those other children follow the same rules), explain that you and the other adult have different rules for your respective children. However, try to avoid these problems by attempting to keep the rules for all children the same, within the limits of their ages, during visits. For example don't insist that your child make her bed if the other children don't have to make theirs. If the other kids go to bed later, your child shouldn't be made to stick to an earlier schedule unless she's much younger than her counterparts.

Of course sometimes you really don't have control over the rules for the other adult's children, especially if you're not remarried. For example your girlfriend might allow her youngsters to use language you wouldn't allow your child to use. In such cases explain to your child that you and your girlfriend have different ways of doing things and that sometimes this translates into different rules for your kids. You want your child to follow your rules: "Elizabeth and I feel differently about this, Candace. I expect you to pick up your toys and put them away after you play with them. Elizabeth doesn't have that rule for Andy, and it's not up to me to tell Andy what to do. I know you think this is unfair, but I still want you to do it."

Issues involving stepchildren, half siblings, or your significant other's children can get very complicated. The important thing is to give your child permission to tell you whatever is bothering her about these relationships. Then discuss the matter calmly, explaining your reason for doing things the way you do them. The point is to keep the lines of communication open and to let your child trust that she can discuss her thoughts, worries, and feelings with you without your becoming angry or defensive.

MORE SUGGESTIONS

1. There are a number of excellent children's books about divorce. You can read one to a younger child or give one to your older youngster to read himself. These books are helpful because they point out thoughts, feelings, and fantasies your child could be having but might not talk about with you. If you read the book together, you have a great opportunity to check out whether or not your youngster is having a particular problem.

2. As with adults, it's helpful for kids who share a common problem to have a support group. Many schools, churches, and community agencies have such groups for children whose parents are separated or divorced. By being with other youngsters and hearing their similar problems and concerns, your child will feel less alone.

3. It is a good idea for you (and your ex, if possible) to have a consultation with a mental-health professional after a separation, divorce, or remarriage. This is especially true if your child shows continuing signs of adjustment problems, such as regressive behavior (tantrums, bed-wetting), a drop in grades, depression, anxiety, or aggression. Psychotherapists are trained to pick up on issues that you, your ex, or your child might need to address. An objective evaluation of your situation and recommendations for dealing with it can prevent more serious problems later on.

5
Sickness/Death

WHEN YOUR CHILD HAS TO CONFRONT SERIOUS ILLNESS OR DEATH EITHER IN someone he loves or in himself, your heart goes out to him. It's hard enough for adults to face these things, much less a child.

With illness at least there's hope of improvement or recovery. Death leaves no options and might be especially difficult for you to discuss because you understand its finality.

Preschool children's concerns about death are different from those of school-age children. The young child is primarily concerned with separation issues. He worries literally that he won't be able to see, touch, and hear the dying person again. If it is *he* who is dying, he worries primarily about being away from his parents, other people he loves, and his pets.

An older child is usually more afraid about the process of dying. If someone he loves is dying, he wants to know if that person is in pain. If *he* is dying, he fears the physical assault of hospital procedures and the pain he might feel as he dies. He's not likely to focus on the finality of death the way an adolescent would, since children typically don't even begin to understand the abstract notion of the finality of death until they are about eight or nine years old.

Even if your child has no personal experience with death, he's likely to become curious about it by age four or five. He'll see dead animals in the road and hear about fatal car accidents on television. He might have confronted the death of a beloved pet, or he might know a child at preschool who has had a death in the family.

If your child must confront critical illness or death in either himself, a pet, or a person she loves, encourage her to talk about it. You might think you'll protect her from emotional trauma by not bringing up the subject until she does, but it's best to get things out in the open so that she can vent her feelings. It's okay and even healthy for her to cry or to be upset when these matters are discussed, so clearly give her this permission.

Remember that emotional wounds are similar to physical ones: You can clean them up and put bandages over them. While they might look nice, they're likely to be festering underneath if they're deep. What's really best is to drain the wound. This process might be painful, but then it's ready to heal properly, from the inside.

1. I DON'T WANT TO GO TO A HOSPITAL! DO I HAVE TO GO?
   Why can't you just take care of me?
   What's an operation?
   Does an operation hurt?
   Will they put me to sleep? How?

Children are understandably afraid of hospitalization. After all, their routine is totally disrupted, they're put in a strange place among people they don't know, they're given food that's different from what they're used to, they're confronted by scary things, such as tubes, needles, bedpans, and strange-looking machines, and they're subjected to uncomfortable if not painful medical procedures.

All children will experience anxiety about going to a hospital. They often show regressive behavior, such as clinging, wailing, bedwetting, nightmares, sleep problems, and fears of being separated from a parent. Preschoolers in particular can be enormously frightened, since their distinction between fantasy and reality is more blurred than is the case with an older child.

It's very important to prepare your child for any planned hospitalization. Even though he's likely to become anxious when he hears about it, youngsters who've been prepared have less anxiety during hospitalization, fewer complications, and a faster recovery. With a preschooler you'll want to tell him a day or two ahead of the event; to contain his anxiety, you don't want to give him too much advance warning. An older child needs to be told about a week ahead of time.

Let your child know she's having to go to the hospital because the doctors and nurses there can help her get well or feel better. Some things need to be done that can't be done in a doctor's office or by a parent; hospitals have special equipment and medicines that you don't have.

Reassure your child right away that you'll be with her all or most of the time she'll be in the hospital. If your child is a preschooler, either you or the other parent should stay overnight with her unless the hospital doesn't allow it. Even older children feel much less anxious with you there at night, so arrange to stay if at all possible. Children are terrified of abandonment, and that's exactly what it feels like to them if you leave them alone at night. If you must leave, explain to your child exactly when you'll return. It also helps to leave something special of yours with her, such as a piece of your jewelry, a picture of you, or any item of yours that has special significance for her. You might also consider asking a relative or friend (someone the child likes) to be with your youngster when you or the other parent can't stay.

Give your child a clear explanation of exactly what's wrong with him and what will be done about it. Tell him what a hospital room looks like, how he'll go to the bathroom, and what he'll be wearing. Tell him about any procedures you know he'll experience (blood tests, shots, X rays, IVs) as well as a description of what will be done for his particular illness.

If your child will be having an operation, tell her about the operating room and that she'll be getting an anesthetic: "Carrie, there is medicine called an anesthetic that will let you go into a special sleep where you won't be able to feel any pain while the doctor is fixing your throat. You'll wake up when it's all over." Children are very concerned about how they'll be put to sleep, so find out before the surgery how the anesthetic will be administered so that you or the doctor can answer your child's questions.

If surgery is involved, tell your child he'll have an incision (a cut) and stitches, which he'll be able to see when he wakes up. Sometimes parents leave this information out, and the child wakes up terrified when he sees evidence of the incision. Young children have little understanding of their inner body parts and may fantasize that something's been removed that hasn't been, that their insides were pulled out, or that they'll burst open and everything in them will come spilling out. When you clearly tell them where a cut will be made, the reason for it, and how the stitches mend permanently, their fears can be kept to a minimum.

If your doctor is willing, ask him to talk to your child about the operation before it occurs, perhaps using drawings to explain what the surgery will involve. This helps your child to build rapport with the doctor and to feel more confident that the doctor is going to help solve a problem. It also helps right before the surgery to have your child meet the nurse who will be present when your child comes out of the anesthetic, ensuring that your child will wake up to a familiar face.

Make sure your child doesn't expect to feel fantastic when he wakes up after the operation is over. Explain what he will experience in terms of postoperative pain or discomfort, but make sure he realizes these problems do go away and that he'll feel better each day: "Mark, when you wake up from your operation your throat will be very sore. You probably won't want anything to eat for a couple of days, but you'll be able to have liquids and ice cream. The doctor will also give you some medicine to help your throat feel better while it's healing."

Don't lie to your child. If you know something will hurt, tell her: "Yes, Melissa, shots do hurt a bit, but just for a short time." If you are honest about what is painful, your child will trust you when you tell him that something *doesn't* hurt: "X rays don't hurt, honey. There's a machine that's like a big camera; it takes pictures so that the doctor can see what's inside your body. It doesn't hurt a bit."

In addition to preparing your youngster for the negative aspects of being in a hospital, be sure to include the positives: "Max, there's a playroom there with lots of toys you can play with while you're getting well, Aunt Joan and Uncle Billy will be coming to visit you, and you'll get presents from some of the people who come to see you."

If your child has a chronic illness or medical problem that is likely to result in a series of hospitalizations, deal with the one coming up. But if he asks if he'll have to go back, be truthful without overwhelming him: "Yes, honey, you might have to go back again later on. We need to see how this operation works, and then we'll know more about whether or not you'll need to go back."

For the child needing medical tests, tell him, "The doctors need to do some tests that can only be done in the hospital. These tests will tell us more about what's happening to your stomach so that the doctors will know how to help you feel better."

If your child has to be hospitalized in an emergency situation, you'll not have had time to prepare him. Explain what you know is happening or will be happening as you become aware of it. An honest "I don't know, honey. We have to wait to see what the doctor says" is better than speculating or making promises you can't keep. Support the hospital staff and take your cues from them. After the emergency is over, explain to your child what happened and why things were done the way they were.

2. WHY DID THIS HAPPEN TO ME?
Why did I have to be born sick?

Although these questions are about illness, the answers would also fit for youngsters with physical or mental disabilities. The child's feeling of being a victim or of being different from her peers can be the same whether she is ill or handicapped.

When something negative happens to us, we all eventually ask ourselves, "Why me?" Kids are no exception. The problem is children often imagine that their illness represents punishment for something they did wrong.

Youngsters with a chronic medical problem such as epilepsy, asthma, diabetes, or cystic fibrosis do feel that they are different from their peers. They may require special diets, frequent visits to the doctor or the hospital, and/or restriction of activities other kids take for granted.

Make sure your youngster knows she did nothing wrong or bad to cause the problem she's having. You might tell her, "Honey, you were just born with this problem and we really don't know why or how it happened. But I can tell you that you did nothing to cause it. Many people are born with these kinds of problems, and it's just one of those things you have to accept."

If you do know the reason, tell him, "John, when you were little, you were very sick and had a high fever. The doctor thinks that's what caused you to have seizures." Or, "Honey, asthma seems to run in our family. Just like you inherited your musical talent from your grandmother, you probably inherited your asthma too."

Let your child know she's not alone in wondering why she is stuck with some chronic problem most other people don't have. Sometimes parents are so focused on helping a youngster accept her condition that they unwittingly give her the message "it's no big deal." The youngster is either put in the position of having to deny her normal feelings of frustration, sadness, or anger or she simply feels misunderstood and unsupported. Encourage your child to express her feelings about being "different" and let her know you sympathize with the problems her condition creates for her.

3. IS MOMMY GOING TO DIE?
Why does Daddy keep going to the hospital?
Will you get sick too?
Why do people have to die?
Why did Mommy die?

The way you answer this question if the person asked about is sick but is expected to recover will be different from how you'd respond if that person has a life-threating illness or is dying.

QUESTION ASKED ABOUT PERSON WHOSE LIFE IS NOT THREATENED

When a parent or someone in the family becomes ill or has to go to the hospital, children might wonder if that person is dying. Reassure your child by telling him what is wrong with the person and that the person is getting treatment or an operation to correct the problem. Let him know: "Honey, most people don't die until they are very old."

If your child mentions someone who wasn't old and who died, say something like "Yes, your Uncle Kirk was pretty young, but he had a very bad illness that can kill people. Your mom doesn't have an illness like that; she's having an operation to fix the problems she's been having with her stomach, and she's going to be just fine."

QUESTION ABOUT PERSON WHO HAS A LIFE-THREATENING ILLNESS OR IS DYING

When your child asks about someone who has a terminal illness, even if it's you, be honest without destroying hope. When he says, "But couldn't Mommy die?" it's best to say, "That is possible, Jeremy, but Mommy is taking some treatments that the doctors are hoping will help her get well" or, "Honey, people can die from what Mommy has, but the doctors have lots of medicines they're going to give Mommy to try to help her get well."

Realize that whichever parent is critically ill, your child will probably want to know if the other parent is going to die too. She'll also want to know who's going to take care of her if she has no living parent. Answer these questions directly rather than pushing them aside with statements like "Honey, that's ridiculous! Of course I'm not going to die!" You might say, "Amanda, I'm in perfect health and probably won't die until I'm very old. But if I did, your mother and I have arranged for you to live with Aunt Minda and Uncle Herb. They love you and would take very good care of you."

At the point when it is certain the person is actually in the dying process, tell the truth: "Honey, the doctors have done all they can to help your dad. Yes, he is dying." Let the child see the person if he wants to, but don't force it. Tell him what to expect: what the person looks like, whether or not the person can talk coherently, what tubes and other equipment the child will see.

If you are dying or know you will die in the near future, talk to your child about it, if possible, if she's over five or six. Difficult as this conversation will be, it will strengthen the bond and the trust between you. Let her know what you treasure about her, how much you love her, and who will be taking care of her. Tell her you know she'll miss you and will be sad, but that you want her to have a happy life and not to stay sad because you can't be with her. You love her, and you've shown her how to love others. Reassure her she did nothing to cause your illness or death. Even if she's been mad at you lately, she doesn't have to feel guilty about it, because you've always known she loves you.

You might also want to write your child a letter so that she'll have it to read after you die or when she's older. A letter can be reworked until it says exactly what you want to get across. Or you might consider making a video for your child to view at a later time.

Whether in a conversation or a letter, be careful what you ask of your youngster. Children can feel enormously guilty or burdened if you make specific requests of them that they can't or don't want to fulfill. For instance it wouldn't be wise to say, "Always take care of your daddy for me," or, "Don't ever quit your piano lessons," or, "Keep going to church every Sunday for Mommy."

If your child wants to visit a person who's close to death, encourage him to tell that person good-bye even if the person seems unconscious or is uncommunicative. While this is an extremely sad situation for everyone involved, your child will be better off knowing he said "I love you" and telling the person good-bye while the person was still alive.

After a loved one has died, your child might ask you why the person died or why anyone has to die. Give your youngster a factual explanation of the illness or circumstances surrounding the person's death ("He was in his nineties and died of old age").

If your child is asking the more philosophical question about why people die, explain that death is part of life, a natural process. When people will die or how they will die is usually an unknown. Tell your youngster any religious beliefs you have about death that will be comforting to him, such as concepts of an afterlife or reincarnation. If you haven't settled these issues for yourself, tell her, "Honey, that's a pretty heavy question, and I'm still trying to figure out what I believe. This is something you'll decide for yourself when you grow up."

4. I KNOW GRANDPA'S SICK. BUT DOES HE HAVE TO BE SO MEAN?
Why do you spend all your time with Grandpa?

When someone in a child's family is ill, especially if that person lives in the child's home, the emotional dynamics of the family change. Typically a parent is required to give more attention to the ailing member. While children might understand the need for this, they're still likely to resent the inconvenience of having someone ill at home as well as the fact that their parents can't spend as much time with them as they would like.

Let your child know you understand her frustration, anger, and jealousy of the time you or your mate must spend with the ill person: "Honey, I know you love Grandpa and want to help take care of him, but I also know it's very hard sometimes. Even though we all want to help him, there will be times when all of us will get angry about this situation because we have to change so much of our normal routine." Or you might say, "Boy, I really get upset when Grandpa yells out and expects us to just drop what we're doing and go do something for him. Don't you ever feel that way?" By acknowledging that it's okay to be angry about this situation, you give your child permission to feel his own anger without feeling guilty about it.

Often people who are ill have personality changes that can be very disruptive. They may become highly irritable, unreasonable, childish, self-pitying, anxious, depressed, or confused. Be clear with your child that you find these things aggravating also. Help your youngster not take it personally if the ill person is critical or irritable with her: "Barbara, when Grandpa jumps on you about leaving your dishes in the sink, just remember he's grumpy with all of us sometimes. Just tell him you're sorry and don't worry about it. Okay?"

Your child is likely to feel particularly guilty if a sibling is seriously ill. A part of him will be very jealous of all the special attention the other child is getting. Instead of waiting for him to bring it up, take the initiative and tell him, "Honey, I know your dad and I have been spending almost all our time with Ben since his operation. I wouldn't blame you for feeling angry about it sometimes." Reassure him you love him and that you want him to feel free to come to you and tell you when he feels he's being left out or forgotten.

5. WHAT IF DADDY'S AIRPLANE CRASHES?
Could Peter have gotten out of that fire if he'd tried harder?
Couldn't I be killed in a tornado?

People die in all kinds of accidents and natural disasters. As children become aware of this fact, they might begin to worry about something like that happening to them or to someone they love. While you want to be truthful when your child asks you about these things, you don't want him to become preoccupied with or fearful of the possibility of accidental death.

When your child asks you if some disaster or accident could happen to her, to you, or to someone she cares about, tell her, "Yes, Darlene, something like that could happen, but it's not very likely." Go on to explain any factors that help ensure the safety or unlikelihood of the situation she's worrying about.

For example: "Your dad has been scuba diving many times and has taken classes to know how to do it safely." "If a tornado were coming to our city, the weather forecaster would warn us so that we could go to the part of the house that is safest." "Airplane pilots are highly trained and have lots of flying experience before they're allowed to be commercial pilots; it's really very safe to fly, even though you saw that accident on the news." "We have smoke alarms on our ceiling so we'd know right away if a fire had started and we could get out safely." "Honey, there have been thousands of earthquakes throughout the years, but very few have killed people."

Your child might ask if people who have been victims in an accident could have done something to prevent their own death. She might think the person could have tried harder, been smarter, or performed some superhuman effort. If so, she'd feel less vulnerable because the accident would seem controllable in some way. The truth is that no matter how smart, how determined, how strong, or how good a person might be, that person can still be a victim in an accident or a disaster. In other words bad things can happen to good people.

If you have religious or philosophical beliefs that might comfort your child, share them with her: "God has a plan for all of us. When someone dies, it may seem terrible to us, but God has a reason for this even though we don't understand it." Or, "Honey, the Universe has a reason for everything; we just don't understand what the reason is."

Help your youngster see the futility in worrying about things over which a person has no control with an example from her everyday experience: "Theresa, people have been known to fall in the tub and break a leg while taking a bath. Now, do you think we should all stop taking baths because we're worried that might happen to us?"

Encourage your child to be alert and to practice good safety precautions. Let her know that this is the best way to minimize her chances for accidents.

6. WHAT HAPPENS TO PEOPLE AFTER THEY DIE?
   Where do dead people go?
   Can Daddy see me?
   When I'm dead, will I get to see Daddy again?
   What does it feel like to die?
   Do people who are dying know it?

Many of your answers to these questions will depend on your own spiritual beliefs. However, there are certain basic facts about death that need to be explained to all youngsters.

Whether or not you believe in a soul or an afterlife, there is no dispute about what happens to the physical body. When someone dies, the physical body deteriorates. The person no longer breathes, thinks, feels, has a heartbeat, or moves. And once a person is dead, his body doesn't come back to life.

Explain to your child how our society takes care of the physical body: "Kenny, the people at the funeral home will put Grandmother in a special box called a casket. Then the casket will be buried in a hole in the ground at a place called a cemetery. A cemetery is a pretty, quiet place where people bury the people they love."

If the dead person is to be placed in a mausoleum, you'll need to explain that the casket will be put in a special large vault, like a drawer, inside a cement or marble structure. The vault is sealed, and the body remains there. If the body is cremated, tell your child something like "Since the person feels no pain when he's dead, the body is burned into ashes; the ashes can be scattered where the person wants them, such as in a river or in some especially pretty place, or they can be buried in a grave or placed in a mausoleum."

If your child wants to know why a body has to be buried or cremated, tell her we show respect and love for a person by doing this. It's a natural process for the body to disintegrate slowly and turn to dust.

When you're telling your child your religious beliefs about what happens after a person dies, let him know that people have different ideas about it. After all, nobody really knows what happens. What you are telling him is what you believe. Discussions about the soul, an afterlife, heaven, hell, whether or not you'll see people you've known, and whether you'll be born again should be based on your personal beliefs (see Chapter 13).

When your child asks what it feels like to die, there is some information you can draw on. Many people who have had "near death" experiences report that there was an incredible sense of peace and love surrounding them and that there was no physical pain. Many tell of a beautiful white light, which they interpreted as God or some spiritual figure or cosmic force, coming to meet them. This information might be very comforting and reassuring to your child.

The other answer is simply, "Honey, I don't really know what it feels like. I wish I could tell you, but I can't." You might ask your child to tell you what *she* thinks it might feel like to die, reinforcing any of her positive thoughts by saying, "That sounds lovely, honey."

7. DO I HAVE TO GO TO THE FUNERAL?
What if everyone is crying?
Do I have to look at a dead person?

Funerals and memorial services can serve an important psychological function by allowing loved ones to say good-bye to a dead person and to accept the reality of his death. It's not uncommon for people who did not go to some sort of ritualized service after a death to have difficulty realizing the person actually died.

Understandably you might wonder if a child should attend a funeral, given the sadness and high emotion of the situation. You might be concerned about your child's reaction to the corpse if there is an open casket or a viewing, and you might feel uncomfortable about her witnessing adults crying or sobbing.

A preschooler can be very frightened and confused if he sees adults expressing intense grief. Also, many young children have nightmares about dead bodies and fears about going to sleep after they attend a funeral, especially if they view the body. For these reasons it is not generally recommended that preschoolers attend funerals. However, you might want to have your young child draw pictures with you to "say good-bye" to the person who died.

If your preschooler hears you talking about going to the funeral and asks what it's about, tell her you're going to church or synagogue for a special service in honor of the deceased. If she wants to go, tell her this service is only for grown-ups (and older children, if she's aware of an older child who is going). Instead of taking her to the funeral, help her draw pictures with you about things she remembers about the person who died and help her to "say good-bye" in her own way.

If your child is six or older, tell her in specific terms what to expect at the funeral. This would include a description of exactly what will happen, where the body will be and how it will be displayed, what will be expected of her, and how other people are likely to react (for example, sobbing). After you've explained everything and answered her questions, give her the choice of going or not going: "Some people feel that going to a funeral is the best way to say good-bye, but some people find it way too sad and prefer to say their good-bye in a different way, perhaps alone. What would you like to do, honey?"

Accept your youngster's decision in spite of your own preference. Reassure her that you know she misses and loves the person who died whether she decides to attend the funeral or not.

Some parents don't offer their school-age children a chance to go to the funeral, thinking they'll spare their youngsters a traumatic experience. The problem is that children may feel very guilty long after the funeral is over if they didn't join everyone else in saying good-bye. This is why it's important to listen to your child carefully and help him formulate whether or not he wants to participate.

If your child chooses to see the body, either in a viewing or at the funeral, she should be accompanied by an adult who's not going to become upset. Some children want to touch the body; some don't. Take your cue from your child and let her know that whatever she does is okay. Never force her to do or to say anything against her will.

If your child is viewing a body, you might quietly ask him if he wishes to say something to the dead person. If he chooses to say nothing, tell him, "Grandmother knows you love her very much, Stephen."

Let your child know it's perfectly okay and natural to cry when someone dies, either when talking or thinking about them or during the funeral or memorial service. Don't try to suppress your own tears in an effort to be strong for your child; instead model for him that crying is a healthy form of emotional release. However, make sure he understands that you can't measure the amount of a person's grief by whether or not that person cries: "Will, you'll see some people crying, but not everybody cries. Even if a person doesn't cry, it doesn't mean he doesn't love your grandmother or that he's not very sad she died."

Know that your child might worry that she caused the loved one's death, especially if she had been angry and perhaps wished something bad would happen to that person. The younger the child, the more likely she is to believe in such magical thinking. To help your child understand that angry feelings toward someone don't cause that person to die, use yourself as an example. Let her know that you had both positive and negative feelings toward the person who died and that you're having to deal with both: "You know, honey, I really loved Grandma, but sometimes I got very angry with her. Now that she's dead, I wish I hadn't gotten mad at her as much as I did. But we all get angry with people we love, and I know she knows how much I really loved her. Have you ever had any of these feelings?"

If your youngster lets you know she's struggling with guilt about angry feelings toward the person who died, tell her directly that her thoughts did not cause the person to die: "We all get mad at people we love, honey; sometimes we even wish something awful would happen to them because we're so mad. Of course if something bad does happen, we feel terrible because we really love them and didn't really mean that thought. Don't ever worry that those angry thoughts could really make someone get sick or die."

Realize that it's hard for children to tolerate intense sadness or anxiety. Typically they'll express themselves by becoming more physically active rather than talking about their feelings. They might also have dreams about the dead person or even claim to have seen the person in a vision. It's important not to worry that the child's insistence that she "saw" the person is a psychiatric problem or to try to talk her out of her perception. Simply accept her vision as a sign of your child's positive feelings for the deceased and help her to interpret the event in a positive manner.

Your child might initially deny a sense of loss and act as if the person's death doesn't bother him. When he does admit his grief, he might tend to do it in small doses. He might cry a little while and then run off to play. Acceptance of the reality of death and the grieving that goes with it takes a long time, perhaps even a year or two. However, if your child has negative behavior changes or continues to be overtly upset by the death of a loved one a month or so after the death, consultation with a mental-health professional is recommended.

8. AM I GOING TO DIE?
   Will I ever get well?
   When am I going to die?

The answer to these question depends of course on whether your child is basically healthy or whether she has a life-threatening illness.

QUESTION WHEN CHILD IS HEALTHY

If your child is well and asks if she's going to die, explain that everyone dies, but that most people don't die until they're very old. Find out why she's worried about dying and deal with her concern. Be alert for signs that she's feeling guilty about something she's done or thought about doing and is worrying that she'll die as a punishment.

If your child is sick but doesn't have a life-threatening illness, reassure her that the type of sickness she has doesn't kill people: "Honey, chicken pox is something lots of kids get, and adults too. It makes you feel pretty bad for a while, but it goes away in a week or so. You're going to be just fine."

QUESTION WHEN CHILD HAS A LIFE-THREATENING ILLNESS

Know that youngsters by the age of six can sense when they are critically ill and that they may die from their sickness. They pick up clues from their parents, their doctors, and the medical staff, despite the adults' efforts to behave in a cheerful, normal manner. If they spend much time in the hospital, they realize that other children, often their friends, have died of the same illness they have. When children can communicate their fears and feelings about their illnesses and about dying, they feel less isolated and lonely.

If your child brings up his approaching death, or the possibility of it, discuss it with him truthfully and lovingly: "I can understand about your worrying you might die, Russ. You do have a serious illness, but the doctors tell us there are still many things to do that can help you get well and medicines to take that can make you feel better."

In addition to telling your child about medical procedures that might help him, let him know that he can do some things to help himself. He can cooperate with the doctors and nurses by doing what they ask, and he can learn relaxation skills to help with pain control. Letting him know he can help himself in these ways gives him some sense of control over his life, combatting the feeling of helplessness that can be so overwhelming in such circumstances.

This is the time to ask your child what he thinks about death and to tell him your beliefs. If you believe there is a spirit within him that will live forever, tell him. Hard as it is, ask him what specific fears he has about dying and reassure him appropriately: "Yes, honey, if you die, the doctors will give you medicine so that you'll be comfortable." "Yes, if you die, you can certainly be buried in your jeans and favorite

T-shirt." "Yes, if you die, I'll give your baseball-card collection to your cousin."

If your child is seriously close to death and there is clearly no hope left and she asks about dying, acknowledge that there is no more the doctors can do for her illness but that they will do everything to keep her as comfortable as possible until she dies. Reassure her of your love and of all the special things about her. Comfort her with any religious beliefs you have, such as "You are going to be with God," or, "Don't be frightened. You're going to a wonderful place called heaven where there is love, peace, happiness, and no more pain," or, "You're going to join God; know that we will always love you."

If you do not have religious beliefs, let your child know she will be free of pain when she dies and in total peace. Reassure her that you will love her forever.

9. WHY DO PEOPLE KILL THEMSELVES?
   What is suicide?
   Is it bad to kill yourself?

Since elementary school children do think about and actually commit suicide, you'll want to be sure your child isn't asking these questions because she's thinking of ending her own life.

If she asks about suicide because someone she knows or heard about tried or succeeded in killing himself, she's wanting to know why another person would deliberately end his life. If the reason she's asking isn't obvious, don't be afraid to check it out by asking, "Have you ever thought about killing yourself, Randy?" If you ask this question calmly, your child will be more likely to tell you the answer.

QUESTION MOTIVATED BY GENERAL CURIOSITY ABOUT SUICIDE

Let your child know that a person who deliberately ends her own life (unless that person has a terminal illness or is very elderly) is a very troubled person. This doesn't mean the person is crazy; rather the person was feeling very hopeless about her life for some reason.

However, be clear with your child that suicide is a very angry act (again, with the exception of a person facing a terminal illness or a very elderly person). In reality that person is telling the people who love her that she's rejecting them. However, she might not have been consciously aware that her suicide was a statement of anger.

Let your child know that even though sad, unfair, and upsetting things happen to everyone, most people don't kill themselves as a result. The person who decides to commit suicide has never learned how to cope with feelings of anger, disappointment, sadness, hurt, or fear. To counteract the notion that suicide is a heroic act, let your child know that it takes much more courage to live and face problems than it does to kill yourself.

Tell your youngster that suicide is tragic not only for the person who died but for the people who love that person. Loved ones not only have to deal with the person's death but they'll ask themselves if they somehow caused the person to kill himself. A person wonders, "Did I do something to make this happen?" or, "Could I have done something to stop this from happening?"

Reassure your child that a suicide is *never* the fault of anyone else. Instead it's due to a serious personal problem of the person who killed himself. While suicide itself is tragic because it hurts so many people, the person who does it isn't bad; the person is just troubled.

QUESTION MOTIVATED BY CHILD'S OWN SUICIDAL THOUGHTS

If your child tells you she's been wishing she was dead or has been thinking of killing herself, ask her to tell you her reasons. Why is she so unhappy? Has something happened she's afraid to tell you about because she's afraid you'll be mad or that she'll get someone in trouble? What is she telling herself that's making her feel so hopeless?

Let her know you want to help her with any problem she has, even if the problem is her relationship with you. Reassure her that everyone has problems but that there are ways to work them out. Most important, tell her how much you love her and that you never want her to kill herself. Hold her and comfort her. Then make an appointment for a consultation with a mental-health professional for further advice.

MORE SUGGESTIONS

1. To prepare your child for hospitalization, you might take her to visit the pediatric ward of the hospital before she's admitted. Check with your hospital to see if they have special preadmission visits for children. There are also a number of children's books that deal with topics of illness and hospitalization, which can be helpful.

2. When a loved one dies, older children can sometimes release their feelings by writing or dictating a "letter" to the dead person. It should include anything the person did that made the child angry, all the things the child loved or will miss about the person, and

anything else the child wants to say. Encourage your child to tell the person good-bye at the end. This process can be very helpful in releasing your child's emotions.

3. You might help your child commemorate the loved one's memory in a personal way. He might plant a tree in the person's memory, make a collage of pictures of the loved one and display it, hang something on the wall of his room that reminds him of the person, do some volunteer work for an organization that was special to the deceased, draw a special picture and frame it—the list is as limitless as the child's creativity.

6
Crime/Violence

IT DOESN'T TAKE LONG FOR YOUR CHILD TO FIGURE OUT THAT NOT EVERYONE plays by the rules. Almost as soon as she realizes there are laws and standards of conduct, she sees and hears about people breaking them.

Your youngster will also learn very quickly that her world is not always safe or loving. She'll see the news on television, hear your conversations about current events, and listen to her peers talk about scary things that happen, including parents who commit violent acts on their children. Words such as *rape, murder, mugging*, and *assault* are likely to become a part of her vocabulary in the elementary or even preschool years.

At about age four, children typically become worried about monsters, sharks in the bathtub, and other scary things that they fear will cause them harm. When the younger child hears about violence, he'll try to relate it to his own personal life. He'll worry if *he'll* get shot, if *his* mother will be attacked, or if a robber will come to *his* house.

The older youngster is more capable of broadening his concerns to include people outside his own family and circle of friends. He might question the motives of people who commit crimes and violent acts, even feeling some empathy toward them.

It's critical to make it clear to your child that there's a huge difference between violent *feelings* and violent *actions*. Feelings, even violent ones, are neither bad nor good; they just exist.

If Johnny's sister makes a nasty wisecrack about him at the breakfast table, Johnny might well feel like hitting her or throwing food at her. To do so, however, would get him into big trouble.

You need to let your child know that it's perfectly normal for a person of any age to have violent thoughts or feelings when he's angry—and this includes being mad at Mom or Dad! It's not uncommon for a youngster to have an occasional moment when he wishes his mother would get run over by a truck, his dad would fall down the stairs and break his leg, or his baby sister would meet with some terrible fate.

Of course if one of these awful things did actually happen, your child would feel very sad about it. But he shouldn't have to feel guilty about his earlier aggressive wishes or fantasies for fear he caused the event to happen.

You'll want to let your child know that angry thoughts do not make violent events happen. It's true, there are rare circumstances in which a person is legitimately unable to control violent impulses. For example he might have a brain tumor or be high on drugs. Basically, however, violent acts occur because a person chooses to behave in a violent way.

1. WHY DO PEOPLE STEAL?
   What's so wrong with taking something from stores? They have lots of stuff and they make lots of money. It was just a pack of gum! What does it matter?
   If somebody's poor, why shouldn't he be able to take something he needs?
   Why can't I take Daddy's change? You do.

You can help your child begin to develop a sense of property ownership in the preschool years. Teach him that some things belong to Mom and Dad and that he can't play with or use them without permission. If he has a brother or sister, let him understand that some toys belong exclusively to him and some belong to his sibling, but some are to share. In the case of friends each controls his own property and decides when to share it.

When your youngster wants to know why some kids steal, tell him there are several reasons. If the child is very young, she might truly not understand what stealing is. Or a youngster might know that stealing is wrong but might decide to do it anyway because she badly wanted the item and doesn't have the money to buy it. An older child might feel insecure about her popularity and steal because she thinks the item will bring her status with her peers. She also might steal out of a sense of rebellion; she's angry about rules and decides to break one just to prove nobody can control her. Or she might even get a sense of pride out of being clever enough to steal and get away with it. A youngster might also steal from a parent because she feels a lack of attention from that parent; having something personal that belongs to the parent symbolically helps her to feel closer to that parent.

As you are explaining the possible motivations for stealing, make it clear that such behavior is wrong and illegal. The fact that a person does it, however, doesn't necessarily make that person bad. It might simply mean he or she has a problem and needs help solving it. The stealing is a symptom of the underlying problem.

Let your older youngster know that even if someone is stealing for one of the above reasons, that person probably is unaware of exactly why he's doing it. After all, we all sometimes do things without consciously knowing the reason. If our behavior becomes a problem and we can't seem to stop it, we might go to a mental-health professional to figure out what our inner motivation might be and what we can do to change.

If your child wants to know why it's wrong to steal from a store, don't jump to the conclusion he has a character problem or that you have somehow been remiss in shaping his moral development. Realize that he sees stores as having lots of money and might find it hard to understand why it's such a big deal to take something without paying for it. You might tell him, "All the things in the store belong to the person who owns that store. The owner has already paid for his merchandise, and it's his until someone buys it from him."

While your child might readily see the error in stealing costly items, she could still wonder what the harm is in stealing something that's inexpensive. "Honey, whether it's a package of gum or an expensive watch, it still belongs to the person who owns the store. He paid for it and it's his until someone buys it from him. The price doesn't matter."

It also helps to give your child an example she can relate to. Tell her, "Molly, let's say you got a lot of money from your grandmother and you went shopping. You might buy some expensive things, like a stereo or some outfits, but you might also get some cheaper things, like barrettes or bubble bath. Now, you'd be angry if someone stole any of those things, even the cheaper ones, right? If something is yours, you simply don't want anyone to take it without your permission."

Your child might raise the more difficult issue of a person's being poor, "needing" the item and then taking it from someone who isn't poor, presuming that that person can buy another one. "It still belongs to the person who bought it, whether that person is rich or not" might be all the explanation necessary for the younger child. For the older youngster you might explain the relativity of "being rich": "To you, Larry, that little boy you're talking about is poor, but *you* might seem poor to another kid whose parents have a lot more money than we do. Does that mean it's okay to take things from anyone who has more money? Of course not. If it were, pretty soon we'd all be stealing from somebody, and nobody would ever be able to own anything or to trust anyone!"

Explain to your child that there are organizations that help very poor people obtain food and other necessities. In fact your youngster might want to volunteer for a church, school, or community project that collects items for people who can't afford to buy them. But not having something doesn't give any person the right to steal it.

If your child wants to know why he can't help himself to your money, realize that he might not see this behavior as stealing because it's "all in the family." If you take your spouse's change from the tray on the dresser or go into his wallet, your child might figure that she should be able to do the same. Let her know, if it's true, that you and your spouse consider that money as joint property, something you have agreed to share with each other, just as your child and her brother have declared the video-game machine as something they both share. In other words people decide what to share and what not to share by mutual agreement.

2. WILL ROBBERS COME TO OUR HOUSE?
   Why did the robbers break in to our house?
   Will the burglars come back and hurt us?
   Were the robbers watching us?

Answers to your child's concerns about robbers or burglars are obviously going to depend upon whether your family has had a personal experience with them.

WHEN YOUR HOUSE HAS NOT BEEN BURGLARIZED

If your child has heard about a burglary, she might worry about your family becoming a victim of the same crime. While you need to answer honestly that it's possible for any family to experience this event, you'll want to help her feel as secure as possible about her safety.

Let your young child know about the normal precautions your family takes to keep anyone from breaking into your home as well as any safety features in your house. Show her how you lock doors and windows and teach her how to do the same thing when she's old enough to learn. Remind her of your proximity to her when she's asleep and let her know that your first priority in any type of emergency would be to get to her and keep her safe and close to you.

With an older child, particularly one who will be home alone at times, make sure she knows the procedure for locking doors and setting the security system if there is one. Teach her how and when to call 911 (or other emergency number for your community), and post a list of important phone numbers of your office, relatives, and neighbors by your phones in case she needs to reach someone quickly. If she's coming home from school and no one will be home, teach her not to enter the house if she sees someone in the house, finds the door lock broken, or opens the door and finds that things have been scattered around. Tell her to run to a nearby neighbor's house (or to some other previously agreed-upon place close by) in the event that she feels it's unsafe to enter the house.

WHEN YOUR HOUSE HAS BEEN BURGLARIZED

Your child will naturally feel frightened whether or not he was at home when the burglary occurred. He'll worry that it could happen again and that family members or pets could be harmed. One of his worst fears has come true: that he and his family really aren't safe anymore.

Before a burglary kids usually think their home is a refuge, a place where everything and everyone is protected from anything bad happening. With a break-in that fantasy is shattered. Your goal as a parent is to help your child feel as safe as possible without denying the reality of what did or can occur.

Answer your child's questions about the burglary honestly, but at the same time give reassurance about the future. For example you might say, "Maria, of course it's possible that we could get robbed again. But we've done some things now that will make our house safer. We've gotten an alarm system (we have a special new lock for the front door, we're going to keep our dog in the house at night so that his barking will wake us up if someone tries to break in, we've put locks on our windows, your dad fixed the back gate, etc.)."

Realize that if your older child is used to coming home from school when no one is at home, she might feel frightened to continue this plan after a burglary. Plan to have someone at home (or ask a neighbor to come into the house with her) for a few days until she once again feels comfortable with her usual routine.

It helps to explain to a child that people who try to steal things from your house usually are not trying to hurt anyone. In fact most burglars don't want people to be at home when they rob a house, and they try to pick a time when nobody will be there. They just want to take what they want and get out. People usually get hurt only if they forcibly try to stop the burglars. This explanation can help calm your child about his fear that you or he will be killed or hurt by robbers.

Of course, your child might be old enough to realize that it's becoming more common for burglars, especially if they're on drugs, to senselessly kill or wound their victims. As with any other senseless crime or accident, admit that such things do happen, but give your child any information that would help him realize that such things are unlikely to happen to him or your family: "That has never happened in our neighborhood, Alan; it's happened only in a dangerous part of town," or, "The police in our city are really working to end the drug problem," or, "Honey, tragic things like that can happen, but they're very rare; just know that your mom and I will always do the very best we can to keep us all as safe as possible."

"But why us? Why did they rob *our* house?" your child might wonder. What she's asking of course is for an understanding of how criminals select their victims.

Tell your youngster that burglars often don't even know who they're stealing from. They pick one house over another for different reasons: They think it will be easy to break into or they notice nobody is home and the neighbors are away. Or they might figure your house looks like the kind that would have nice things that burglars want, like TVs and VCRs.

If you have reason to suspect that your house and family had been watched in order for the burglars to determine your living pattern and pick their best time to break in, your older child might pick up on your suspicion. Acknowledge that it's very scary to think someone has been watching you, as this is a real invasion of your privacy. But help your child see that a burglar who was watching was doing so to find out when would be the best time to break in, when no one was home, not because the burglar was trying to harm anyone or was plotting against your family in some personal way.

When your child asks about the possibility of the same burglars returning, tell her it's very unlikely. "Honey, the burglars already got what they wanted here; why would they come back?" or, "Now the burglars know that we've probably done some things around here to make it much harder for them to get in. They'd be stupid to come back here."

3. How Do You Know Somebody Won't Set Our House on Fire?

When a youngster understands the destructiveness of fire and that there are people who set fires, she might be frightened that someone could set fire to your home. Since arson is commonly motivated by revenge or deep personal hatred, let your child know that there's nobody who hates you or no reason for someone to want revenge upon you: "Sol, people who set fire to another person's house are people who are mentally very sick and who hate that person and want to hurt that person. Your dad and I don't know anyone like that; we don't have any enemies, so we don't have to worry about someone setting fire to our home."

4. If Someone Hits Me, Should I Hit Him Back?
When should I stand up for myself and when should I give in? What do I do when a bully picks on me?

You don't want to see your child come home with a black eye or a bloody lip. Nor are you likely to want him to be aggressive and get into fights. But you don't want him to be a wimp, either, as this sets him up for lower self-esteem and for ridicule from others. So how do you teach him to know when he should stand up for himself and when he should just walk away or give in?

When your youngster asks about hitting someone back who's hit him first, help him understand the difference between hitting as a physical attack and hitting in self-defense. "Frank, I've told you it's not good to get into a fight with someone, because there are better ways to solve problems. And I wouldn't want you to *start* a fight with anybody. However, if Bobby hits you, I think you might hit him back rather than just walk off. Sometimes you have to stand up for yourself and show a bully he can't push you around without your fighting back. Even if you don't win the fight, Bobby will think twice before he picks on you again. Lots of times when you call a bully's bluff by showing him you're not afraid of him, he'll back off." Obviously if Bobby is a much larger child or older child, you would advise your child differently: to get out of the situation as best as he could without running the risk of getting seriously hurt.

When your child wants to know how he should decide whether to stand up for himself or whether to give in, tell him his response really depends upon the situation. His first priority should be his physical safety, so if he's outnumbered or if he's confronted by a much bigger or stronger child who wants to take something from him, the best thing is to comply immediately with what the group or child is wanting him to do. If he resists, threatens to fight, or is verbally provocative, he increases the chance he'll get hurt. Reassure him that in this situation giving in is the smart thing to do. Also let your youngster know that this situation is one that he should tell you about; this is not a time for your child to be brave and try to tough it out on his own.

More typically, however, your child is likely to find himself confronted by a bully. Although you might be tempted to suggest, "Ignore him!" this strategy rarely works. If your child continues to ignore a persistent bully, he'll probably invite the bully to pick on him more.

You also want your youngster to learn to take care of himself emotionally as well as physically. Sometimes that means standing up for himself even if he risks getting into a physical fight. Tell him his first strategy should be to make some face-saving remark and try to get out of the situation. He could say things like "Come on, Mike, grow up!" or, "Hey, Mike, leave me alone!" or even, "Listen, Mike, we don't need to fight about this."

But if the bully challenges further by insisting on or starting a fight, let your child know he'll have to make an important decision. Will he feel better about himself if he fights, even if he loses? Will he not only have more self-esteem but also gain admiration from his peers for not "wimping out"? Or will he end up feeling less than good about himself because he's likely to get totally trounced? Let your child know he's the only one who can make this decision, rather than advising him to "stand up for himself" no matter what the outcome.

You might also consider giving your child more confidence about his ability to defend himself by enrolling him in karate or boxing lessons. The feeling of being able to take care of himself physically, even if it's never tested, can help your youngster's self-esteem and decrease his fears about physical attack.

5. WHAT'S SO BAD ABOUT JOINING A GANG?
   Why do kids join gangs?
   What's a "drive-by shooting"?
   When gangs want to fight, why doesn't anybody just say no?

Resist your urge to show shock and horror that your child would even ask why it's bad to join a gang! Instead try to tune in to why your youngster would ask this. Perhaps he's lonely, feels he doesn't belong, and is wanting a way to have guaranteed friendships. Being in a gang might sound pretty appealing to him. Or maybe he's just trying to "push your buttons" by saying something he knows you'll think is outrageous.

Either way your child will be more likely to listen if you explain your point of view without getting emotional. Since gang membership is on the rise (even among suburban kids), you can't assume your youngster will be protected from becoming involved in a gang just because you live in a particular neighborhood, go to church regularly, or volunteer at school.

Tell your child that kids join gangs for the same reason that people join clubs—to belong. Those kids think they're getting lots of friendly buddies to hang out with, but what they really get is quite different. Unlike organized clubs, gangs typically identify themselves with some negative purpose. Youngsters frequently have to do something violent or illegal to become a member; once a part of a gang, they might have to continue to do antisocial acts.

Let your child know that one of the bad things about getting into a gang is the loss of individual freedom. A person must be obedient to the gang leader no matter what he himself wants to do: "If the gang decides to commit some crime and you don't want to take part, you have no choice. In order to be part of the gang and avoid possible severe punishment from other gang members, you have to do it."

Even scarier is the fact that many gangs don't allow a person to leave the gang. "Chad, a gang might hurt or even kill you or a member of your family to get revenge for your leaving it. They do this because they know that you know too much about the activities of the gang, so you could tell authorities like the police about the bad things the gang has done."

If your child asks what a "drive-by shooting" is, explain that it's an activity gangs use to get revenge on people. "A car filled with gang members drives by a person's house, or some other place where the gang knows he'll be, and the gang members shoot him." Explain that usually the victim is known to the gang, although sometimes the shooting is totally random and represents the gang's violent rebellion toward innocent people.

When your youngster wants to know why kids just don't say no when they're in a gang, explain how difficult it is for a child to do that. Gangs thrive on intimidation and fear; if one child wants to disagree with the gang's plan, that youngster feels helpless because the other gang members might hurt him if he doesn't go along with them. Also let your child know that when people act as a group, events can happen very quickly. Individuals can get caught up in the energy of the group and do things they'd never think of doing if they'd been alone or had more time to think about it.

Tell your youngster it's normal to want to feel that she belongs and has friends. There are all sorts of groups and clubs based on positive interests and activities that she can feel proud to join. Let her understand that gangs rarely turn anyone down so long as that person is willing to be totally controlled by the gang. This is why kids who feel they don't fit in with any group are easy prey for gang membership. In positive groups people still have the right to exercise their own judgment and personal preferences, and they don't get threatened, hurt, or killed if they decide to leave the group.

6. What Does *rape* Mean?
Why do people rape people?
Can a boy get raped?
What's "date rape"?

If your child asks about the meaning of *rape*, your answer will depend upon whether or not she knows what words like *sex* and *sexual intercourse* mean. If she's too young to know what sex is, tell her, "Leslie, rape is when a man touches a woman's body in ways she doesn't want him to," or, "That's when a man forces a woman to let him touch her bottom (or whatever words you use for genitals) with his penis."

If she's old enough to know what *sex* or *sexual intercourse* means, you could say, "That's when a person forces another person to have sex (sexual intercourse)." However, resist the temptation to explain the act of sexual intercourse to your child at this time if she doesn't already know about it, even if she's old enough to know the facts. You'll want to wait for a time when you can talk about intercourse in the context of making love rather than in a discussion about a violent act.

When your child wants to know why rape occurs, make it clear that rape is about power and control, not really about sex. Sex is just used as the vehicle for committing violence. Rapists are either mentally ill or are very self-centered people who use sex as a way to control, hurt, or humiliate another person.

"Kenny, *rape* means when a man forces a woman to have sex with him against her will. It's a very violent, mean thing to do to someone. Sex is supposed to be one way to show a woman you love her and that she's very special to you, not a way to get power over her or to hurt her."

When your youngster asks about males being raped, you could tell the younger child, "Yes, a boy can get raped if a man forces the boy to let him touch private parts of the boy's body." For the child who's old enough to know about anal intercourse, you might say, "Yes, honey, boys and men can get raped. Since males don't have vaginas, the rapist puts his penis into the other man's rectum." If your youngster wants to know if women ever rape men, explain that it's possible for a woman to force a man to have sex with her, but very unlikely.

When your child asks about date rape, realize that the question provides a good opportunity for you to give either a son or a daughter some valuable preventive advice. Explain that while many rapists don't even know their victims, in date rape a boy and girl agree to go out on a date and the boy wrongly assumes he has a right to have sex with the girl in spite of her feelings. He might think her no really means yes because he doesn't listen to her or thinks she's just playing hard to get. Later he can't believe the girl thinks he raped her. Or the boy might deliberately decide to ignore a girl's wishes because he thinks, for some reason, that she *should* have sex with him.

Let a boy know he should never force a girl to have sex under any circumstances. Even if she's agreed and then changes her mind, he should always heed any remark that suggests a no. Also, if the girl has been drinking heavily, a boy would be taking unfair advantage of her to have any kind of sexual contact with her unless the girl had willingly agreed to having sex with him before she began drinking.

Let a girl know she needs to be very clear with a boy when she says no so that there isn't a chance he'll interpret this to mean yes. She should never give double messages, such as saying no when she's really teasing and inviting the boy to continue being sexual with her; if at some point her no becomes real, the boy might not believe her.

Also tell your child that date rape almost always occurs when one or both parties are using alcohol. This is another good reason why neither a boy nor a girl (or a man and a woman) should put themselves in a vulnerable situation by drinking alcohol (or using it excessively).

7. WHAT SHOULD I DO IF SOMEBODY TRIES TO GET ME TO TAKE DRUGS?
   Should I tell on someone who offers me drugs?

You might be shocked that your elementary-age child would ask you about being offered drugs. The harsh truth is that many youngsters this age are being solicited to take drugs by an older child, teen, or adult.

Just telling your child to "say no to drugs" is not enough. You also need to understand how your child might be feeling as well as the peer pressure he might be under. Realize that he might be very frightened of the person who approaches him and be afraid to come right out and refuse the offer. That person might even be someone your child looks up to or wants to please, and it might be very hard for him to turn that person down.

So you'll want to talk with your child about the difficulty he might feel in saying no and give him some alternative ways to refuse if he's not comfortable doing so directly. For example, he could say something like "I already take medicine and I can't mix it with anything else," or, "I'm allergic to lots of drugs, so I can't experiment with them." Realize it takes a very confident child to state clearly, "I don't believe in taking drugs," or even, "I don't do drugs."

When your child asks if he should tell on someone who offers him drugs, let your child know that taking or selling drugs is both illegal and dangerous. Make it clear that no matter what the person offering the drugs says or who he is, even if he's a family member, your child should tell you about it. Acknowledge that your youngster is violating that person's confidence by giving you the information. Tell him you know it's a hard thing for him to understand, but he's actually helping that person in the long run by turning him in. That person is not likely to seek help for his problem until he's caught; when he's caught, he might choose to get professional help. Reinforce the fact that your child is not really doing that person a favor by letting him continue to use or sell drugs.

8. Why Would a Mother or a Father Hurt Their Own Child?
Is it ever the child's fault when a parent abuses him?
Who helps kids when their parents hurt them?

When your child hears about child abuse, she naturally wonders how a parent could do such a thing to his or her own child. Children think their parents can do no wrong; indeed part of the process of growing up involves realizing that parents are human beings who have problems of their own. Adults lead complicated lives that can be very stressful, and they sometimes displace their frustrations onto their children. They might also have emotional or character problems that get in the way of their parenting abilities.

Tell your child that a parent who repeatedly abuses a child has serious emotional problems. It's very likely that parent was abused herself when she was child, and she hasn't learned to handle anger and frustration in an appropriate way. There are also parents who lose control of their anger and become momentarily abusive on only one or a few occasions. Such parents typically feel very guilty afterward because they're basically not violent or mentally ill.

If your youngster asks if abuse is ever the child's fault, tell her clearly that it's never okay for a parent to abuse a child. While a child can sometimes be very provocative, disobedient, or disrespectful to a parent, it's the adult's responsibility to maintain control over his own behavior.

Realize that your child might be asking this question because she fears that you or her other parent might lose control and become abusive. This idea might seem preposterous to you if your youngster has never experienced any form of abuse from you or anyone else. However, if you (or the other parent) are fairly volatile, have a hot temper, yell a lot when you're angry, and/or have body language that conveys rage, realize that the intensity of your anger is very frightening to your child. Know that it's very natural for him to fear that you just might lose control and become abusive. If you (or the other parent) have this type of temperament, reassure your youngster that you might seem scary when you're mad, but that you will not lose control.

If your child wants to know where abused children can get help, tell her that there are laws that make adults responsible to report abuse if they know of it. Often a doctor, teacher, or principal finds out or suspects that a child is being abused and reports it to the police or to state authorities. The child might tell that person about the abuse, or that person might notice unusual bruises or marks on the child's body. The police or agency looks into the matter by questioning the child and the parents and getting help for the family.

9. WHY DO PEOPLE KILL OTHER PEOPLE?
   Is it ever okay to kill someone?

It's important to understand what your child is asking in posing these questions. Is he afraid someone is going to kill him? Did he hear about a murder on the news and wants an explanation about motives? Is he feeling angry and afraid that he might lose control and hurt someone? Has he had a fantasy or dream that he killed someone and is scared that this will come true?

Often you'll know the reason behind your child's question because of the context in which she asked it. If you're not sure, ask for information: "Why do you ask?" or, "Have you been thinking a lot about this? How come?" or, "What made you think of that, honey?" are ways you might explore your child's concerns.

QUESTION TAKEN AT FACE VALUE

Let's assume your child has heard about someone killing another person and is asking why anyone would do such a thing. The younger child will probably be satisfied with "A person who kills someone else is very sick."

You might need to explain further: "I'm not talking about the kind of sickness when a person has a fever and has to take medicine or get a shot from the doctor. This kind of sickness has to do with a person's feelings or emotions. All of us have angry feelings at times, and we might even wish that someone else was dead. But the person who really kills someone doesn't control these feelings."

"Why doesn't he?" your child asks. Explain, "Honey, there could be many reasons, and those reasons could be very complicated. Although we might not know what the reason is, we know we could find some reason if we had all the necessary information." You don't want to answer with "We just don't know why people kill people," because your child might conclude that people kill willy-nilly and that anyone could commit murder at any time without any reason. If your youngster presses you for more information about reasons why a person might kill someone, you could add, "It might be because of something that happened to him when he was a little boy. Maybe he grew up very mad because someone was very mean to him."

Some older youngsters will have more detailed questions about what makes people so emotionally troubled that they would kill someone. You might tell them, "Many people learn to be violent because of the way they were raised. They might have grown up with parents who beat them or abused them. Or they might have lived in a neighborhood where people shoot, beat up, or knife other people. The grown-ups who lived with them did not teach them the value of human life."

The older child might bring up situations when killing is sanctioned by our society. If she asks if it's ever okay to kill somebody, explain, "Our laws tell us you can kill someone when they're trying to kill or seriously hurt you or someone else. It's also legal to kill your enemy when your country is in a war and to kill some criminals who are in prison for committing violent crimes." Of course, after explaining how and when our laws justify killing you'll want to discuss your values on issues of self-defense, war (see Chapter 7), and capital punishment (see Question 10) if they differ from the legal view.

Older youngsters might also understand the concept that sometimes really nice people end up committing a violent act because they're in a situation where they're unable to use good judgment and they have poor impulse control. Violent acts performed when someone is high on drugs is a perfect example.

QUESTION MOTIVATED BY FEAR OF GETTING KILLED

If your child's question seems to be caused by fear of being killed, he needs reassurance rather than an explanation about the motives behind killing. You might give him a hug, saying, "Don't worry, honey, you're safe." Sometimes this kind of authoritative, affectionate response is all that is needed to calm your child.

If he persists with his concern, you might need to respond to the content of his fear. For example, if your young child heard on the news about a child who was killed in another town or state, you could tell him, "That happened in a place that's very far from here, Tucker." Even if the killing took place just around the block, it helps to remind your youngster, especially if he's a younger child, of the distance between where the killing occurred and where your child lives.

QUESTION MOTIVATED BY FEAR OF LOSING CONTROL

For the child who's afraid of losing control of her own angry impulses, you can reassure her that people can be very angry and still not kill or hurt someone. Even if she's dreamed or fantasized about killing someone, she needs to know that such images don't mean she's going to do it. What they do mean is that she's angry at someone or something, and the dream or fantasy is a good way of calling attention to this so that she'll be more aware of her own feelings and can do something about them. Ask her what she's so angry about and offer some options for her to release her anger in an appropriate way (see "More Suggestions" at end of this chapter).

Realize that when a child tells you she wants to kill someone, her meaning is much different from that of an adult who says the same thing. The child doesn't really want the person to be dead; she just wants that person to go away and be out of her life momentarily to relieve her own feelings of anger, pain, or suffering. Knowing this fact will help keep you from worrying about the possibility your child is having murderous impulses toward someone she simply doesn't like or want around at the moment.

10. WHAT IS CAPITAL PUNISHMENT?
What's an electric chair?

For the young child you might only need to tell him, "That's a type of punishment for prisoners, honey." When your child is ready to know more, tell him that in some states there are laws that allow capital punishment for prisoners who commit very serious crimes, such as brutal murders or other extreme acts of violence. *Capital punishment* means the same thing as *the death penalty*; the prisoner is put to death for the crime.

Explain that each state has a specific way that a prisoner is killed. Some are given an injection (shot) that kills them and some are sent to an electric chair. "An electric chair is a special chair that has been wired to give a person such a large jolt of electric current that it stops the person's heart and he dies." Since children worry about whether or not something "hurts," explain that in both death by injection and in death by the electric chair, the person dies quickly and with very little pain. Let your child know that this punishment is controversial. Many people think that certain serious crimes should be punished by death; others think that there's nothing that justifies the deliberate killing of another human being. As with any moral issue, explain your beliefs to your youngster and tell him why you think the way you do.

MORE SUGGESTIONS

1. Since violence occurs because people allow their anger to get out of control, it's important to teach your child how to release anger appropriately. Active methods for a child to vent anger include drawing a picture of the person he's mad at and then scribbling all over it, jumping up and down on it, or tearing it up. Or he might want to throw something safe, like a pillow, against a wall in his room. He might pretend his pillow is his mother, the school, the world, or whatever he's mad at and beat it on the bed or the floor. Also, both younger and older kids may like to make a "Mad Bag" out of a canvas duffel bag or pillowcase. This bag can be stuffed with soft material and should be large enough for the child to straddle, but not so big

that it's too heavy to move. When a child is angry, he can beat on this bag to vent his frustration.

2. An older child might like to use a technique relied upon by many adults to release pent-up emotion in a more passive way. She might keep a journal or diary, which nobody but she will read. Sometimes just putting what she's mad about into words can help release the pressure.

3. If you think your child might be frightened of your anger, make a deal with her. Tell her that when you notice you're becoming intensely angry, you'll go to another room to cool off. You might also encourage her to tell you when she's getting frightened by your behavior so that you can either pull yourself together or leave the room until you regain your composure.

4. Remember that the best way to help your child learn to cope with anger is to be a good role model for her. Do some of the things when you're angry that you're asking her to do: draw, write, listen to soothing music, go for a walk, work out, take a time-out, or simply talk to her calmly about your feelings.

7
War/Disaster

Most of the time when your child is scared, you feel some sense of control over the situation. Even if you or your youngster is facing a life-threatening illness, at least you have medicines and medical procedures that are a source of hope. But if you're facing war or a disaster such as an earthquake, flood, fire, hurricane, or tornado, it's natural to feel overwhelmed yourself. The magnitude of the threat to human life and the unpredictability of events is so great that your own heightened anxiety spills over to your youngster, making it difficult for you to give genuine reassurance and comfort.

For a child the thought of being permanently separated from a parent is terrifying. This is why she'll have abandonment fears if a parent goes to war or if a disaster, or the threat of one, occurs. Although your child hopefully will not have to confront war or a disaster, if she watches television, she'll be exposed to reports of these events from all over the world and is likely to have many questions about them.

For example, when she hears a news story about an upcoming hurricane, she'll be worried about how close its path is to her house. When she sees children starving in Third World countries, victims of earthquakes and villages ravaged by war, she might become very frightened that the same things will occur in her own neighborhood. Some children are able to view these situations and realize that they are occurring in other parts of the world or are of no immediate threat. Other youngsters are unable to make this distinction. Since television is your child's primary means of hearing about such events, it's important that you become an "in-house censor" and monitor what she's viewing in order to keep her from developing unnecessary anxiety.

When our country is actively participating in a war, such as the Gulf War, your child will probably have numerous questions. First and foremost, she'll want to know if you, the other parent, or her older brother or sister will have to go fight in it. She'll be frightened about whether or not the person will come back and what will happen to her if they don't. She'll also need your help to sort out how close the war is to affecting her everyday life ("Will they drop a bomb on our house?"). If your child is older, she might want to know why wars happen, as well as details about war equipment, weapons, and a soldier's lifestyle.

If your family is involved in a disaster of some kind, everyone's first concern will be physical safety. Once the imminent threat is over, both you and your child will be likely to be confused and numb from the shock of your experience. In the aftermath of a disaster it's very important to keep your child with you if you possibly can, rather than letting someone else care for him. To the extent that your child can help, even in some small way, let him. The family's working together to clean up, repair, or help others can serve as an important bond and can provide structure during this confusing period.

After a disaster the sooner you can reestablish your normal routine or create a new one, the better off your child will be. His anxiety will be lessened when he knows what to expect. But he also needs to sort out what has happened and how this event has changed his life. This means he needs to talk, to ask questions, and to vent his feelings.

Whether the concern is about war or about a disaster, your child is likely to have adjustment problems related to her experience. She might have continuing fear about injury, death, separation, and loss. She might show sleep disturbances, including frequent nightmares or the refusal to sleep by herself. She might experience difficulty in school from problems in concentration, or she might attempt to stay home from school altogether. She might become anxious and clinging, or she might become more aggressive or oppositional.

If your child wants to sleep with you after some traumatic event, it's perfectly okay to allow her to do so in order to re-create feelings of safety. Once these have been reestablished, however, encourage her to make the transition back to her own bed.

If your youngster's initial adjustment difficulties after a trauma do not decrease once your life is pretty well back to a normal routine, consultation with a mental-health professional is recommended. The therapist can give you specific suggestions to help alleviate the problem.

Help your child put destructive acts and natural disasters in perspective. Remind her that these are unusual events and that the world also provides many positive experiences.

1. WHY ARE THERE WARS?
    Are wars good or bad?
    Why can't people talk it out instead of fight it out?

When your young child asks why wars occur, you might simply say something like "Because the two countries can't agree and have decided to fight about it. It's a very sad thing."

An older youngster of course will want more information. Explain to her that wars are fought over differing belief systems. Beliefs are something a person feels very strongly about, so if two people get into a dispute, they need to find a way to resolve the problem. Be clear, however, that war is never the only way to solve the dispute.

Explain that one option is simply for the people involved in the dispute to talk with one another about why they believe the way they do. These discussions can lead to greater understanding on both sides, and one side might convince the other side to change its mind because of some new information. Give your child an example she can relate to: "Like if your friend believes all boys are terrible and you don't, you could tell her about some nice things you've seen boys do and perhaps your friend would change her mind."

Then, too, there is also compromise. Two people can try to each give a little so that both people end up winning something. For example, "Let's say you and your friend both spot a toy and each of you thinks it should be yours to play with. You could solve the problem by figuring out a compromise both of you could feel good about, such as one of you playing with the toy for an hour and letting the other person have it for the next hour."

Of course sometimes people just agree to disagree. They accept the fact that they each believe differently, but decide to accept their disagreement and not try to force the other side into changing its mind: "Let's say you and a friend want to vote for different people in your school election. If one of you couldn't change the other's mind, you could decide that you'd each vote the way you wanted, but that you could still be friends."

Explain that when people don't solve the problem in these ways but remain convinced that what they believe is right, they could decide to fight: "When countries, or large groups of people, decide to fight, we call it war. In war people feel so strongly that they're right, they're willing to give their lives to try to win."

This explanation makes it clear to your child that you feel wars are a very bad way to try to solve a problem. They're bad because they destroy human lives, tear families apart, and leave severe physical damage in the area where they're fought.

If your child wants to know why all people don't try to talk things out instead of fighting, let her know that a commitment to negotiate rather than fight is itself a belief. If a person doesn't live in a country, society, or group that values nonviolent conflict resolution, that person will believe that war is an acceptable way to settle disputes.

2. HOW DO YOU DECIDE WHO ARE THE GOOD GUYS AND WHO ARE THE BAD GUYS?
   Isn't it good when one of the bad guys gets killed?
   How come the bad guys don't think they're bad?

Remember, kids are very concrete in their thinking; they really believe that there is a "good" and a "bad" regarding everything. In a conflict they'll think somebody has to be "right" and somebody has to be "wrong."

If your young child asks who the good guys are, he wants to know which side you favor. Simply tell him, "Adam, I want the _____s to win." You might also add, "It's just too bad they have to do it by fighting."

Your older youngster will need you to give him a lesson about human nature. "Honey, the people on each side think they're the good guys. Each side is dedicated to its own cause (beliefs) and thinks the other side is the enemy. That's what's so ridiculous about a war. If you lived in one country, you'd see it the way the people in that country see it; if you lived in the other country, you'd think those people are right."

You might also let your older child know that not everyone on one side in a war necessarily feels the same way about a particular issue. For example, when our country sent troops to Vietnam, many people did not agree that our government was right in doing that. Yet regardless of a person's belief about it, everyone called to war was expected to go whether they agreed with it or not. In other words, when a person is a part of a larger group, he might have to bend his own personal wishes to the decision of the group even when he disagrees. This happens in the business world all the time; a person doesn't like a decision his boss has made, yet he must go along with it because the boss has the authority to decide the policy.

Help your child understand that it's a tragedy when anyone on either side in a war gets killed, simply because it is the loss of a valuable human life. The "enemy" is someone's son, perhaps someone's father, and probably has many friends who will be very sad about his death. Nevertheless when people go to war, the goal of getting the other side to surrender involves the loss of lives. People who support the war might feel glad that someone on the "other side" was killed rather than one of the men or women on their own side.

3. WHAT IS TERRORISM?
    Wouldn't it be better just to give a terrorist what he wants so he won't kill the hostages?

For a child a simple definition of *terrorism* is: "It's when someone uses dramatic, violent ways to scare people into doing what he wants them to do." It's best to use examples that have to do with groups of people in order that your child not become unduly alarmed about someone terrorizing him or the family. You might say, "Honey, if a foreign government is trying to get the United States to do something it wants, it might kidnap some of our important government people and then threaten to kill them if our government doesn't do what it wants."

Tell your child that a terrorist might use different kinds of violence to get what he wants. While he might take hostages, sometimes he'll hurt or kill innocent people. Terrorists thrive on creating fear. Not only do they frighten the victims and the people who care about those victims, but they also scare everyone by making them worry that *they* could become the next victim. Terrorists will do whatever they think will "get" to a person or group in order to have their own way. They have no regard for anyone's laws but their own.

When your child realizes that terrorists often choose their victims randomly and consequently might hurt innocent people, he might personalize the situation by asking, "But, Mom, couldn't a terrorist bomb us while we're at the movies?" You can emphasize the unlikelihood of such a thing happening by pointing out that our government has special security for buildings, airports, and other public places where terrorists are apt to strike. Also, if a known terrorist comes to our country, he's going to be spied on by security people, who can stop a violent act before it occurs.

If your child worries that your family might be the target of a deliberate attack, let him know that your family is not important enough to attract such attention. It's usually families having members who do important government or secret work who are vulnerable to terrorists.

Realizing that hostages are in real danger, your child might suggest that people just give in to a terrorist in order to keep everyone safe. You'll want to explain that sometimes people must stick up for an important principle if they're not to be bullied into doing what a terrorist wants: "Gerald, it would solve the problem right now if our government did what the terrorists want and our hostages would be set free. But then there would be no end to what the terrorists would want next. They would know that they could bully us into whatever they want, anytime they want."

To help your child see this important point, use a familiar example of the same principle: "Mick, think about the class bully who wants another kid's lunch money. If that kid gives the money up, the bully will raise the stakes the next time—maybe asking for more money or the kid's homework. There would be no end to what the bully would demand if the kid just kept giving in. Wouldn't that be a terrible way to live, being scared into doing whatever someone else wants?"

4. WILL THE WAR COME HERE?
Could they drop a bomb on our house?
Where will we go if a war does come here?

The younger your child, the more likely he is to think that anything he sees on the television news is going to happen to him. If he hears about someone dropping a bomb in the Middle East, he might wonder if the next loud sound he hears is a bomb headed straight for his house.

Help your child understand the distance involved in a war being fought in a foreign country. For a young child you might say something like "The country where the war is being fought is very, very far from here, Nathan." You might add other facts like "It's way across a big ocean," or, "It's halfway around the world, honey," or, "If a person could drive there without any stops, it would take over a week to get there." If your child is older, point out the country on a map or a globe.

Your child might persist with "what if" questions, wanting to know what would happen *if* the war came to the United States or to his city. Explain that our military is always watching to see if anyone is planning to attack us and that the United States has very special cameras and weapons to ward off any attacker. If an enemy did get through this network of security, our military are trained and ready to fight to protect our citizens.

Explain to your child how a city would react in a time of war. A general alarm would sound to alert everyone of danger, and all radio and television stations would broadcast instructions through special emergency broadcast equipment. Your family would listen for instructions about where to go for safety, as there is an emergency plan for every city or town. People will be told specific places to go where they'll be as safe as possible. It is for this reason you feel it's unnecessary to build a bomb shelter.

Stress your belief that it's very unlikely a war would come to your hometown in the first place. Stating this clearly and repeating it when necessary will help contain your youngster's anxiety.

5. WHAT'S A NUCLEAR BOMB?
   What if a bad guy or a crazy person gets hold of one?
   Would everybody die if a nuclear bomb went off?

Many parents feel at a loss to talk to their children about nuclear bombs because the results of using them would be so catastrophic. Yet kids become aware of nuclear weapons and do ask questions about them. Parents need to be able to answer questions honestly without destroying hope for the future.

The simplest explanation of a nuclear bomb is that it is the most powerful weapon in the world. When it is dropped, it kills everything within hundreds of miles.

With a young child the message you'll want to give is that if there is a threat of someone dropping such a bomb, you will be there to take care of her. If she's in preschool or school, the teacher will care for her. Remember that her main concern, even in a catastrophe, is that she'll not be left alone. Tell her you are optimistic that nations will learn how to settle their arguments peacefully and without using any nuclear weapons.

Your older child will want more information. Admit that the threat of nuclear war is very scary; then give your youngster information about why you feel there is hope that a nuclear war won't ever happen. Point out that because the threat is so frightening, most nations would not want to use a nuclear bomb because they know the other country would retaliate in kind. Let your child know that millions of people throughout the world are working actively to prevent a nuclear catastrophe from happening. Organizations have been formed worldwide to prevent the use of nuclear weapons, and specific recommendations have been made to reduce nuclear arms.

If your child asks about the possibility of some careless or insane person deciding to use a nuclear weapon, explain that in most countries, more than one person has to be involved in deciding to use a nuclear weapon. Such weapons are kept under tight security, and most governments are too aware of the consequences not to have people constantly checking to make sure one person or group cannot have the power to take such a dangerous action. In the few countries where one person would have the power to make such a decision, that person would also be aware of the devastating consequences of such an action. To proceed probably would be a decision to commit suicide for his own people as well as to kill his enemy.

If your child asks about the likelihood of anyone surviving nuclear war, tell her honestly that such a war would probably destroy most of the world. While terrifying to think about, it's important that children grow up understanding the devastation that nuclear war would have on all people.

Explain to your child that the more people work for peace in the world, the less likely a nuclear war will be. Encourage your youngster to think of ways to promote peace, such as writing a "pen pal" in a foreign country, using world peace as a theme for a school project, or joining some of the organizations that promote peace and keeping up with their literature.

6. WILL DADDY HAVE TO GO TO WAR IF THERE IS ONE?
   Do mommies ever fight in wars?
   What will happen to me if you have to go to war?

For a child a parent's getting killed is probably the most frightening thing he could imagine. If a parent goes off to war, that parent's survival will be his main concern.

Answer your child honestly about the likelihood of you or the other parent going to war if one is declared. Obviously if you know you wouldn't be called, your telling him this information will be a relief. But if there's a possibility you would go to war, tell the truth. If your child asks, admit the possibility that you could get killed, but let him know that you would get special training and have special equipment to keep you as safe as possible.

Once your child realizes you could go to war and could even be killed, his next thought will be to wonder who will be there to take care of him. If you are a one-parent family or if you and the other parent could both be called to serve, let your youngster know whom he would live with until your return. Yes, mommies do go to war as well as daddies, so this possibility needs to be discussed if it fits your situation.

Give your child a sense of control by telling him things he could do for you if you were away from home because of war. For example, you could ask him to keep a scrapbook or journal for you while you are away so that you can catch up on what's happened when you return. He could also write to you or dictate letters, which the other parent could send to you if you were stationed in an area where you could receive mail.

If your spouse goes to war, ask your child to take over some of the absent parent's chores, as this helps the child to identify with that absent parent: "Tommy, Dad used to feed Rover. Could you take over this chore for Dad while he's away?" Again, the child feels some measure of control because he feels he's making a contribution and doing something to help out.

As with any traumatic situation, let your youngster know you would want him to talk to the important grown-ups in his life about his feelings. You want him to know that you are not expecting him to "keep a stiff upper lip" and act like he's not scared or upset; rather you want him to know that talking about his feelings is the best way to help himself deal with any problems he might have.

7. WHAT IF THERE'S A TORNADO (FLOOD, EARTHQUAKE) WHILE I'M IN SCHOOL? HOW WILL I FIND YOU?
   I don't want you to go out tonight. What if there's an earthquake?
   Aren't we safer if we just stay home?

Your child might worry about disaster striking, and as always her first concern is if you or the other parent will be there to take care of her. If you're away from home, she'll worry how she'll find you. If you leave the house, she'll worry what she'll do without your presence should something disastrous occur. And sometimes she'll worry so much about something bad happening that she won't want to leave home. Just like the adult who becomes anxious about going on a vacation because she feels unsafe leaving home, a child might develop the feeling that home is the only safe place there is to be.

Reassure your child that our weather forecasters can usually warn us of floods, tornados, and hurricanes before they occur. This gives us time to go to a safer place if necessary and/or to prepare for the event. Teachers know how to take care of kids in schools if there's not time to get children home to their parents. If you are away from home and hear about a potential problem, you will come home immediately or call the sitter and leave instructions.

You can greatly reduce both your own and your child's anxiety about natural disasters by posting a list in the house of "Dos and Don'ts" that are appropriate for a potential disaster. Discuss them with your child, but don't stop there. Go ahead and have a "drill" for these events, using the analogy of getting ready for a play; the players rehearse so that they'll be more confident of their roles and less nervous when the play actually starts. Drills for fires, earthquakes, tornadoes, and so forth help both grown-ups and children alike with a sense of preparedness and make it less likely they'll panic if disaster strikes.

Let your child know you will not leave him unsupervised or without a grown-up close by who will come to take care of him should you not be around at the time of a disaster. This is why you have sitters or have given your older child the phone number of a neighbor close by who is at home. Reassure your child that you will make phone contact with him as soon as possible if you are not able to be with him if a disaster strikes. He doesn't need to worry about finding you because you know where he is and you will make it your first priority to find him. Also, remind him that you will always leave the phone number where he or the sitter can reach you.

If your youngster becomes preoccupied with worries about what can happen should you or he leave the house, tell him that a person can't live his life in fear that some bad event will occur. The important thing is for a person to learn how to take care of himself, how to be careful instead of reckless, how to use good judgment, and when to ask for help if it becomes necessary. A person should then enjoy his life and deal with anything negative if and when it occurs.

You might also point out grandparents or other older adults your child knows who have survived various disasters. To hear stories of how Grandpa dealt with a hurricane, fire, or other disaster helps your child realize that people can live through these situations without any terrible consequences.

8. IF I'M IN A FIRE, SHOULD I TRY TO SAVE OTHER PEOPLE?
   If I see someone hurt, shouldn't I try to help them even if it's dangerous?
   How could I ever leave Fido to burn up in a fire?

It's a difficult concept to teach a child when he is and isn't responsible for other people when a dangerous situation is at hand. While you want him to think about other people and help them if possible, you want him to realize that his first responsibility in a life-threatening situation is to himself.

Tell your youngster that his first job in a fire is to run for safety. He should yell to any other people who might be able to hear and alert them to run for help also, but he shouldn't spend valuable time searching the house for other people, including you. Instead he should run out of the house and yell for help or get a neighbor. He can then tell that person who might be left in the house and where they might be.

If your child has a baby sister or brother nearby, yes, he should grab that infant or smaller child if he can do so quickly and without endangering himself further. But generally speaking, the rule is to get himself to safety and alert a grown-up who can help.

Children have difficulty understanding why they should not take time in a fire to search for a pet. Give your child specific instructions that she must not do this because of the danger. Reassure her that animals quickly sense danger and can often get themselves out of it more quickly and easily than a human.

Reassure your youngster that your first job will be to rescue her or any other children or pets who are in your house. She must leave this job to you rather than try to do it herself.

9. WHAT IF EVERYBODY IN OUR FAMILY GETS KILLED BUT ME?
   Will I be all alone if I have no family?

While your first reaction to these questions might be to dismiss them as too impossible or frightening to think about, they are questions many children consider, and they deserve an honest answer. As with any frightening situation, it's best to go ahead and ask yourself what the worst possible consequence might be and then figure out what you would do if faced with it.

First, of course, you'd want to talk to your child about why she's asking these questions. Did she hear about another youngster who was in this situation? Is she having nightmares about this happening to your family? In other words you'll want to find out what the source is of her anxiety in order to help alleviate it.

No matter what the source of her concern, let her know whom you've designated to take care of her in the highly unlikely event that you and the rest of her immediate family are killed. If you do not have relatives or friends who have agreed to take on this responsibility, tell your child that children who are orphaned become the responsibility of the state and are placed in homes with other such children until a family can be found to care for them.

Reassure her that she would never remain all alone. There are lots of friendly adults in the world who could care for her and help her to grow up. It is the job of the state to find such a grown-up to look after her until she's an adult.

MORE SUGGESTIONS

1. Teach your child the value of negotiation in conflict resolution. Talk openly about disputes or differences of opinion and then discuss possible compromises or solutions. Take a stand that violence is not an appropriate way to handle problems in the family or the world.

2. In addition to holding periodic fire drills (and drills for any other natural disasters likely to occur where you live), take your youngster to visit a fire station. Such a visit can give her a sense of security because she'll actually see that there are trained firemen and special equipment to handle this kind of emergency.

3. If your child has experienced a disaster, encourage him to release his feelings through drawing, puppet play, or role-play. Children need to release their feelings about traumatic events and will often "play them out" rather than talk about them.

8
Prejudice/Injustice

YOUR CHILD WAS NOT BORN WITH ANY CONCEPT OF PREJUDICE OR INJUSTICE; these are beliefs that a person learns. What this means is that the way your child treats people who are different—racially, religiously, or physically—and her sense of fairness are going to depend in large part on what you teach her. Although your words on these matters will be important to her, your actions will speak even louder.

Of course when your child is older, she can unlearn whatever you've taught her. You yourself might be an example of this process: You might hold some belief now that is diametrically opposite from what your parents taught you. If this happened, it's because you got new information, either from your own personal experiences or from hearing facts or opinions from other people you respect.

If you want your child to grow up without prejudice and with a strong sense of justice, it's easier to teach these notions right from the beginning. Point out prejudicial remarks and make it clear that you think they're unfair. Counter negative statements about other people's religion, race, or physical appearance by giving your child correct facts. If you overhear someone say, "All ___s are lazy," point out examples of ___s who disprove these statements. Encourage your child to make friends with children of all races and religions and to study other cultures or subcultures to understand their unique characteristics.

Even more important, help your youngster understand the psychological underpinnings of prejudice. Putting down people who are different is an attempt to bolster one's own sense of worth and superiority and/or a way to blame other people for problems. Seeing oneself as a member of a privileged group and other folks as "on the outside" can help a person feel a sense of belonging.

Let your child know that she does belong to a large planetary group known as human beings. No matter the color of the skin, the form of worship, or the kind of physical condition that each individual has, this group is made up of people who *all* have feelings of love, anger, sadness, fear, hurt, and joy. Differences are to be accepted, appreciated, and celebrated. And justice is the preservation of the right of all people to be treated with mutual fairness, dignity, respect, and compassion.

1. WHY WON'T THEY LET BLACK PEOPLE INTO THE CLUB?
   Why do some people make fun of Jews?
   Why won't Ted's mom let him play with Juan?

If you've brought your child up in an atmosphere of nonprejudice, she's going to be surprised when she hears about situations where people are excluded or discriminated against because of their race or religion. You might answer the young child's concerns with "It's a sad thing, Alicia, but some people don't like other people because of the color of their skin or because of their religion. I think all people should be treated fairly whether they're black, Mexican, Indian, or whatever, or whether they're Catholic, Jewish, Jehovah's Witness, Buddhist, or any other religion. We need to decide how we feel about people by who they are inside, not by their color of skin or religion."

With an older child you'll need to address the reasons behind the prejudice. This would include some history about prejudice in our country toward specific racial and/or religious groups in spite of the rights guaranteed by our Constitution that all groups be treated fairly and have the freedom to pursue their own culture and beliefs.

Just as important, though, is to help your child understand the psychological underpinnings of prejudice. A person who excludes another because of race or religion is setting himself up as being somehow superior to the person who is being discriminated against. It is as if one group thinks they have "the Truth" and decides not to like or respect any person who believes differently.

A person who sees himself as a member of a "special" group, whether because of his color or his beliefs, also has a sense of belonging that can make him feel secure. But we need to point out that while we all want to feel we're accepted by other people, we need to feel secure enough about ourselves that we don't have to put down other people to bolster our own sense of self-worth.

Let your child know it's fine to form groups of people who have something in common (a particular belief, a special skill, a recreational hobby, a desire for socialization, etc.), but it's unnecessary to consider other groups inferior or to make fun of them. It's also against the law to keep a person out of some group on the basis of race or religion. In other words it's fine to form groups if you're doing it to share, but not to exclude or put down other people.

"Samantha, I want you always to consider any person as a unique human being with something to offer or to learn from. Even if that person believes differently from you about something, you don't have to agree—but you need to respect that person's feelings and his right to have his own point of view, so long as that person is not trying to harm other people."

2. HOW COULD THE HOLOCAUST HAVE HAPPENED?

When your child hears about the atrocity of the Holocaust, he might wonder how six million people could be murdered in concentration camps and the rest of the world do nothing to stop it. Your young child will probably be satisfied with "Because a very mentally sick person got into power in Germany, and nobody could stop him."

When your child is ready for more information, let him know about dictators, especially charismatic ones who are able to convince large masses of people to do whatever the dictator wants. Teach him also about racial self-righteousness: "Honey, Hitler was able to convince people that his race was superior to all others. Although he considered Jews, Slavs, Poles, Gypsies, and other groups to be inferior, it was the Jews who became the biggest targets of his abuse. The Holocaust is an extreme example of what happens when people put down other groups of people and teach hatred and intolerance instead of love and tolerance."

Your child might understandably ask why people didn't just say no to imprisoning and killing Jews and other innocent people. Tell her that many people in Germany did not know that these people were being systematically killed and that the climate of fear brought about by the powerful Nazi party made it unsafe for the German people to find out what was really going on. In our country we have much more freedom than people in Germany had, including the freedom to disagree with our government without putting our lives or our family's lives at risk. As for the rest of the world, they did not know what had happened until the war ended and the bodies of millions of Jews were found in the concentration camps. There were no satellite dishes and television sets in that time, so it was difficult to find out what was happening in other countries.

Of course there were obviously some people who knew what was going on, especially the Nazis who worked in the concentration camps. Why didn't any of them say no? Perhaps some of them were filled with hatred themselves and used the Jews as scapegoats; some probably felt it was their highest duty to follow orders as part of their loyalty to the Nazi cause; and some might have inwardly disagreed with what was happening but knew they and/or their families would be killed if they showed any sympathy for the Jews. This was a complicated historical event, and we will probably never understand all of the reasons it happened.

Help your child understand that choosing the ethical choice sounds easy, but when a person is in a situation where his own family and loved ones will be tortured and/or killed if he dares to disagree, it's understandable that a person might compromise his ethics.

Let your child know that the Holocaust is a very painful lesson for people all over our planet. Its message reaches out across racial, political, and national lines as a reminder to unite humanity in valuing the life of every human being.

3. HE'S SO FAT. DO I HAVE TO INVITE HIM TO MY PARTY?
But she's ugly and she scares me. Why do I have to play with her?

Children can be cruel to peers who are physically different in any way. Kids who are disfigured, fat, ill, or physically or mentally handicapped are often shunned.

Basically you want to teach your child to have compassion and empathy for children (or adults) who are different in these ways. Such youngsters want to be treated normally, not as second-class citizens or as objects of pity.

Realize that your child might be frightened of youngsters who have physical differences, especially people with some sort of disfigurement, such as scars, an awkward gait, or an unusual facial appearance. She's frightened because such conditions make it clear that the body is not inviolate against injury and damage. In other words she becomes aware at some level that the problem she sees in the other child is something that could happen to her.

You can help minimize your child's fears about this by explaining the nature of the "different" child's condition, but it's also important to acknowledge the scariness of such a thing happening: "Honey, Melinda's face is scarred because she was burned in a fire. It's very scary to think about something like that happening." While such a statement doesn't change reality, remember that bringing a fear out into the open can help lessen the anxiety associated with it.

When your youngster rejects another child, help her put herself in that child's place. "Honey, if you were Rusty, wouldn't you feel sad if people wouldn't invite you to their parties just because you had to be in a wheelchair (are fat, stutter, limp, etc.)? Rusty is a person who has feelings just like you do."

Encourage your child to set an example for her peers by being especially considerate of children who are different in some way. You might say something like, "You know, Ellen, many kids are mean to kids like Sam, but you never have to be mean to anyone. If you treat Sam nicely, you'll be showing other kids how to treat him. In the long run if you're thoughtful and kind to others in most circumstances, you'll be someone other kids can respect and trust. Even better, you'll respect yourself; you can look in a mirror and think, *I like the person I see!*"

4. Why Did They Fire Our Teacher Just Because He's Gay? *Why don't some people like gay people?*

Be honest with your child about the fact that people who are homosexual are often discriminated against, particularly in a setting where they work with children. In actuality homosexuals are no more likely than heterosexuals to sexually abuse children, yet many people worry that a gay teacher will seduce youngsters into homosexual activities. Tell your child this fact so that he won't buy into the myth that homosexuals are child molesters.

Of course sometimes when someone in any kind of minority group is fired, an assumption is falsely made that the person lost his job because of prejudice. Teach your child to question this assumption by saying something like "Now, Colin, perhaps Mr. Hammon wasn't fired because he's gay. He could have been fired for a totally different reason that we don't know about. It's really very hard to tell why someone is fired unless you are in a position to know what has really happened."

Encourage your youngster to view gays as they would any other group that is an object of prejudice. Point out that sexual orientation is just one aspect of a person's personality and character and that there are many fine, responsible, talented people who are homosexual.

Even if you have religious beliefs that view homosexuality as immoral, you still want to give your child the message that people with all kinds of beliefs and practices are to be treated with the respect with which you'd treat any human being, whether or not you personally share their thinking or behavior. Prejudice against any group for any reason invites hatred, and hatred leads to all kinds of atrocities against humanity.

5. SALLY GOES TO A PSYCHIATRIST. DOES THAT MEAN SHE'S CRAZY? *Melanie's mom was in a mental hospital. Is her mom dangerous?*

Many people still falsely assume that a person who sees any mental-health professional is "crazy." The truth is that most children, teens, and adults who seek such consultation don't have serious psychiatric problems. Typically kids are taken to therapists because of behavior problems at home and/or school or because they are having trouble handling some family or life stress. Teens and adults might be depressed, chemically dependent, anxious, or having problems understanding something about themselves or their relationships. Fortunately the stigma of seeing a mental-health professional is disappearing as more families and individuals ask for help with life's problems.

Although patients who are treated in psychiatric hospitals might have more serious emotional problems, very few are dangerous to other people, even at the height of their disturbance. Give your youngster an example of why a basically normal person might need to be hospitalized in a psychiatric facility, for example a person who realizes she has a drinking problem and needs help in breaking the addiction or a person who has had some severe stress (fired from a job, loved one died, etc.) and is having temporary difficulty coping with her feelings.

It also helps to give your child information about what transpires in a therapist's office. Basically people talk about their problems and feelings in a place where they feel safe. The therapist might give the client another perspective, might help the client better understand herself or her relationships, and might offer some options for the client to handle her problems differently.

By explaining some common situations in which people see psychotherapists, you'll help your child understand that she shouldn't make fun of or be frightened by anyone who seeks help for a problem: "Wendy, strong people know when to ask for help. It's not a sign of weakness."

6. I'M BETTER AT GYMNASTICS THAN HELEN. HOW COME SHE GOT
   PICKED FOR THE TEAM AND I DIDN'T?
   *I worked harder on that class project than anyone else. Why
   didn't the teacher pick me to tell about it at the assembly?*

Your response to these questions is obviously going to depend on
whether your child's perception is accurate. Is she really better at
gymnastics than Helen? Did she really work harder on that project
than anybody else? Or is she just deluding herself? Your careful listening skills will help you determine your approach.

WHEN CHILD'S PERCEPTION IS INACCURATE

If stark reality tells you that your child is magnifying her own skill
or effort, tell her the truth without making her feel like a failure.
Point out something you can compliment her on and then let her
know why you think the other child was selected: "Maggie, I think
you gave a super performance on the balance beam. You were great!
But I really think Meg was outstanding in her floor routine and on
the rings. I guess if I'd been the judge, I'd have had to pick Meg too."

If you know your child is deluding herself about the magnitude of
her own efforts, gently tell her how she's misperceiving the situation:
"Alexis, I know you spent a few hours working on that project and
you felt you'd done a lot of work. But the teacher said that Bradley
had spent several weekends working on it." Or, if you're unsure how
hard any of the other kids worked, you might say, "Alexis, you really
don't know how much your classmates worked on that project. I
know you think you put in a lot of time on it, but someone else could
have worked even harder."

Be sure your child realizes that hard work does not always lead to
immediate success. There are lots of successful adults who had to
struggle many years before they reaped the benefits of their efforts.
Make it clear that most people who work hard eventually reap some
benefit from their efforts.

Let your child know you understand her disappointment in spite
of her error in perception: "Honey, I'm really sorry you didn't make
the team. I know you're disappointed. But the important thing is that
you competed and did the best you could. I'm proud of you." Or,
"Honey, I'm sorry you didn't get picked to speak at the assembly. It's
disappointing when you think you've really earned something and
then you don't get it."

WHEN CHILD'S PERCEPTION IS ACCURATE

When your child deserves to win or to receive some honor and another child is (or seems to have been) selected unfairly, sympathize with your child's frustration and anger: "Honey, I agree you performed far better than some of the girls who were chosen. I'd be really upset too." At the same time use this situation as an opportunity to teach your youngster that it's unrealistic to think that life is always fair: "Honey, sometimes life dishes out things that just don't feel fair. We just have to accept that life isn't always fair and move forward in spite of it."

If you think that prejudice or politics might be involved in the situation, explain to your child what you think might have occurred. However, be careful to point out that your theory might or might not be accurate; you don't want your child to use prejudice as an excuse when things don't go his way.

At the same time help your child see that being "best" or working "hardest" are just subjective judgments. The winner might have been chosen honestly, simply because a judge genuinely thought she was best: "Honey, I thought you gave a better performance than Janie. But Janie was very good, too, and the judges might have seen something in her routine that you and I didn't see. Even experts have different ideas about what's best."

Make sure your child is aware that she's not the only one who wasn't chosen. After all, other youngsters also had hopes of being selected, might also have done well, and are also experiencing disappointment.

Point out that the real gain in any competition or effort is what a person learns by doing it. Even someone who comes in last can feel good about the fact she tried and can learn the lesson of being a good sport about defeat.

7. WHY DO I HAVE TO PLAY WITH CANDACE? SHE'S SICK ALL THE TIME.
    Abby has AIDS. Should I sit next to her on the bus?

It's common for children to reject a youngster who is ill for fear they'll catch whatever that child has. Kids know you can catch chicken pox and colds, so why not cancer?

Teach your child the difference between contagious and noncontagious diseases: "Stacy, a person doesn't catch cancer from anyone else. Amy's cancer is caused by something going wrong in Amy's body. You can't catch it from her." Likewise explain other noncontagious conditions such as epileptic seizures, asthma, cystic fibrosis, and so on, as your child becomes exposed to youngsters with these conditions.

With all of the publicity about AIDS, youngsters do pick up on the fact that this disease is something people "catch" from others (although only in highly specific ways). Reassure your young child, "Honey, you can't catch AIDS from Jennifer. Treat her just like any of your other friends."

With your older child, explain that AIDS is spread through contact with an infected person's body fluids. This could occur during sexual contact, while using contaminated needles (while injecting drugs or having blood transfusions), or from an infected mother to her child during pregnancy. Let her know that she won't get AIDS from sitting near or touching a child who has it or even from sharing toys, dishes, or school materials.

If you have concerns about your youngster's contact with an infected child or adult, contact your pediatrician, family physician, or AIDS information bureau in your community for up-to-date information. It's also a good preventive measure to teach your youngster that spitting and biting, even in games, are totally inappropriate behaviors, especially considering the serious health risks posed by the AIDS infection.

Help your child empathize with a sick child by pointing out how that child's daily life is different. But let her know, too, that sick children have feelings just like anyone else. They want to be treated as normally as possible.

8. WHY DID I HAVE TO MISS RECESS WHEN IT WAS THE OTHER KIDS WHO WERE THROWING PAPER AIRPLANES IN CLASS? *Tommy's the one who plugged up the sinks in the boys' bathroom. Why did the principal suspend me?*

When your child gets into trouble because of someone else's behavior, she's likely to feel she's a victim of true injustice. The issues of group guilt or of "guilt by association" are difficult concepts for her to understand.

Tell her that when a group of kids is misbehaving, such as in the classroom, it is difficult to know exactly how much each person participated: "Honey, how's the teacher supposed to know who's throwing paper airplanes and who isn't in a roomful of twenty kids?

If she can't pinpoint the trouble to specific kids, the only fair thing she can do is to take recess away from the whole class. But that means some kids will get punished who really didn't participate. I agree it doesn't seem fair to those kids, but it would be even more unfair if she picked out just a couple of the kids when there were lots of kids involved. It's one of those tricky situations when you have to decide what's most fair to the most people."

If your child gets in trouble when he's with one or two other youngsters and they've misbehaved when he hasn't, make it clear that his passive participation also makes him guilty: "Tommy, all three of you boys were in the rest room watching Ed plug the sink. Just because you didn't plug it yourself doesn't mean you aren't guilty. After all, you could have told Ed to stop or left the rest room if he wouldn't listen to you. By doing nothing, you are almost as guilty as Ed."

Make it clear to your youngster that saying or doing nothing implies that she approves of what's going on: "Honey, if I stand by and just watch someone mistreating an animal and don't try to get him to stop, that person is going to think I'm agreeing with what he's doing. If that animal gets hurt or killed, I must share the blame because I could have done something but I didn't."

Let your child know it's hard to stand up for what she thinks is right when her friends are doing something she thinks is wrong: "I know it's not easy, Samantha, but sometimes you have to say no to what a friend is asking you to do when you know it's wrong. If you don't say anything, you can get in trouble for your friend's behavior because you were with her at the time she did it."

9. I WAS JUST LOOKING AT TIM'S WATCH TO SEE WHAT TIME IT WAS! WHY DID MY TEACHER TAKE MY PAPER AWAY FOR CHEATING?
Mary and I just went behind the garage to look for her kitten. Why did her mother get so mad?

Your child will rightfully feel it's unjust if he's falsely accused of doing something wrong. At the same time you'll need to help him understand how he might have set himself up for his actions to be misinterpreted. In other words, he needs to learn to see himself through the eyes of others in order to understand their reactions to him.

If your child asks why he's been accused of something he didn't do and you realize he's left himself open for misinterpretation, help him see how another person could perceive his behavior: "Honey, most kids who are looking over another person's shoulder during a test aren't trying to see his watch—they're trying to cheat. I know it's an awful feeling to be accused of something you didn't do, but I can see why your teacher could think you cheated."

Teach your youngster to try to correct the other person's error rather than just to give up and feel angry: "Have you told Mrs. White you were just looking at Tim's watch and not copying from his paper?"

If your child tries to correct the situation but isn't successful, help him figure out why he might not have been believed: "Honey, maybe your teacher was remembering a time when you weren't truthful with her about your homework. Perhaps that's why she doesn't think she can trust you. One of the things that happens when you lie is that you lose a person's trust, and then they might not believe you when you're really telling the truth. I'm sorry this has happened, but there is a lesson in it for you."

Sometimes your child might behave in a way that causes some adults to feel uncomfortable, awkward, or anxious. If your son asks why Mary's mom was upset because he and Mary were playing behind the garage, let him know that when children go off together where adults can't easily see them, adults sometimes think those kids are being sneaky and doing something they shouldn't. Whether it's smoking, sharing a beer, engaging in sex play, or any of the other things an adult might suspect in such a situation, let your youngster know that such interpretations are common: "So that you won't have this happen again, Eric, be sure to play where grown-ups tell you to play and don't go off to a place where it could look like you're hiding something."

10. WHY IS THAT WEIRD MAN ASKING FOR MONEY?
    Should we give him some money?
    Why don't homeless people just go get a job?

Your child's first contact with a homeless person is likely to be when you're in a public place and he sees someone asking for money. When he asks why someone would do this, explain that there are many people who do not have jobs. To get money, they beg for it from other people.

If your youngster wants you to give money to someone who's begging for it, you might model the principle of charity by giving the person a donation. This gives you an ideal opportunity to talk to your youngster about the pleasure of giving: "Denny, when you share what you have with someone who's less fortunate, it really makes you feel good inside."

If your child asks why you don't give a larger sum, you could explain that you prefer to give your larger donations to organized charities. Those organizations make sure that the money is put to good use, such as food stamps, shelter, and clothing. Organizations can also help more homeless people by pooling your money with contributions from other people and buying large quantities of food and supplies at discounted rates.

If your youngster wants to know why homeless people don't get jobs so they can have money and a place to live, tell her that in tough economic times, jobs might not be available. Also people can sometimes get caught up in a chain of unfortunate events where they end up without a job and with no family or friends to help out. Some people lack the skills for certain jobs, such as being able to read or not having had appropriate training. There are also many homeless people who have serious personal problems that prevent them from getting or keeping a job. These problems often include addiction to alcohol and other drugs or other serious personality or emotional problems.

Let your child know that a person's being on the streets says nothing about that person's being a "bad" or "good" individual. The problems of the homeless are very complicated, and our country's leaders are trying to find solutions to help.

MORE SUGGESTIONS

1. Encourage your child to accept invitations to go to a friend's church or synagogue to visit, or take her yourself. This not only educates her about different religions but also encourages her to respect other people's beliefs.

2. If you hear your child making racial or ethnic remarks about someone, talk to her about it. Let her know why such statements are offensive and make it clear you don't approve of them. After all, example is the best teacher.

3. Teach your youngster to be assertive about speaking up when he sees injustice occurring with his peers. He doesn't have to sound like a self-righteous adult, but he can calmly state, "I don't think that was fair because...." You can model this behavior for him by pointing

out any letters you've written to your newspaper or to government officials in protest over such issues.

4. For an older child rent a video that shows the hero standing up for someone who is a victim of prejudice or discrimination. *To Kill a Mockingbird* and *Rainman* would be good examples.

9
Ethics

WHEN YOU SAY YOU WANT YOUR CHILD TO GROW UP WITH A GOOD CHARAC-
ter, what do you really mean? Probably you're talking about wanting
her to have a system of moral beliefs called ethics.

Moral development, however, is a process. Since young children
think in such concrete terms, their view of what's right and wrong
starts out being very rigid. Black is black and white is white, and
there's no gray in between. There is no such thing as an extenuating
circumstance or a degree of guilt. Ask a six-year-old what he'd recommend as punishment for a crime and you're likely to get an eye-for-
an-eye kind of answer. In his young mind there is no hesitancy about
meting out a swift punishment for an offender no matter what the
context of the crime. To the young child unfairness is a matter of not
getting what he wants. Asking him to put himself in another person's
place or to consider another person's feelings is impossible for him.
While you might instruct him to consider someone's feelings as part
of socializing him, realize that his cooperation comes from following
your instructions rather than from a genuine ability for empathy.

As a child matures and becomes more capable of abstract thinking,
he can begin to get a broader picture of a situation. At age eight or
nine he begins to realize that answers aren't so clear and simple
anymore. His thinking becomes more flexible, and he is more likely
to be able to see both sides of an issue. He becomes more compassion-
ate, less self-righteous, and is able to feel empathy. His concept of
unfairness also begins to match that of adults.

As a parent you can help in this developmental process by gently
pointing out a more flexible way of looking at a moral issue. Give

him another point of view, another perspective, which focuses on consideration of the feelings and needs of everyone who's involved. Teach him the Golden Rule as a way of helping him to put himself in another's shoes and to recognize the human strengths and weaknesses in all of us. Realize that he's not going to "get it" on the spot; his development in these areas will be a process rather than a sudden awareness.

1. I Saw Tommy Cheat on a Test. Should I Tell the Teacher? *Why should she get an A and I get a B when she cheated and I didn't?*

While you probably think classroom cheating is absolutely wrong, the fact is your youngster might see this behavior as "no big deal." Kids even brag about the clever ways one can cheat and brush off the matter with "Everybody does it."

You'll naturally want to counter this attitude and will emphatically tell your child not to cheat. The dilemma occurs when your child asks what to do when he knows a peer has cheated. Your answer will depend on whether your child passively witnessed the cheating or was an innocent victim of the cheater. What will happen if he tells the teacher? If he doesn't tell, how do you help him with his outrage at the unfairness of the cheater making a higher grade? And how do you help him understand the reasons a child might feel tempted to cheat?

WHEN YOUR CHILD IS A PASSIVE WITNESS

While your immediate reaction to your child's question might be "Of course you should tell your teacher!" think for a minute about the impact of this advice. If you spotted a person in the grocery store sampling a few grapes, would you tell the manager? If one of your coworkers took an office tablet home and never brought it back, would you inform your boss?

Probably not. Not that you would condone the behavior or encourage anyone to do it. But there are limits to an individual's responsibility for the behavior of other people. The line is usually drawn when someone is doing something dangerous to himself or others or committing a crime. For example, you'd want your child to report another youngster who's starting a fire in the coatroom or a classmate who's hiding a gun in his backpack. But you probably wouldn't consider someone's illicitly munching a few grapes or taking a tablet as significant enough to call it a crime. You'd leave it to the store manager or boss to discover the guilty party. As for the child cheating in elementary school, it might be best to leave that discovery to the teacher, unless the offender's cheating blatantly continues.

The point is you want to teach your child not to take on unnecessary responsibility for her peers' behavior. On the other hand you do want her to have a code of ethics and to stand up for that code when it's appropriate to do so.

In addition, let's face it: The last person other kids like is a tattletale. Tattling is just not a good way to win or keep friends, and you don't want to encourage your youngster to tattle unless it's a necessity.

Suggest your child mind his own business about Tommy's cheating, and let nature take its course. Let him know that teachers are not naive about cheating and will eventually spot a chronic offender. Talk with him about the fact that Tommy is actually hurting *himself* by his cheating.

WHEN YOUR CHILD IS AN INNOCENT VICTIM

You don't want your child to ignore cheating that implicates her. To do so would imply that she is encouraging this behavior or is in cahoots with the offender.

"Tommy, please don't cheat off my paper. I don't want either of us to get in trouble" is a clear message to the cheater. If Tommy persists, he can be told, "I'm going to tell the teacher if you don't quit copying off me."

This tactic lets Tommy know your child doesn't approve of cheating and warns him of the consequences for repeating the act. You might also suggest that your child offer to meet Tommy during recess or after school and talk with him about the material he didn't know.

Should Tommy ignore the warning and your child needs to speak to the teacher, encourage her to do so in private. This is a good time to discuss the courtesy of not saying negative things to or about other people when there is some uninvolved person listening. Your child can understand this when you explain, "You wouldn't like it if I corrected you in front of your friends."

The younger child might not know how to get a private hearing with her teacher: "Just tell the teacher you would like to talk to her alone" will help her get started.

What if your child is afraid of offending the cheater? This peer might be a high-status classmate, her best friend, her only friend, or a bully. At this point you'll need to move the discussion to the importance of people standing up for what they believe is right even if someone gets mad about it. Easy to say, not so easy to do!

Let your youngster know that you're aware how difficult this situation is for her. In this way you reinforce the fact that she's becoming a stronger person for standing up for what she believes. Let her know you'll be very proud of her for taking this risk, perhaps sharing a time in your childhood when you had to stand up to someone and feared rejection or ridicule.

WHAT ABOUT FAIRNESS?

Your child might say, "But, Mom, Michael got an A by cheating, and I did all my own work and got a B. That's not fair!" Obviously your child is right. The situation isn't fair.

At this point you'll need to remind your youngster that the cheater might seem to be getting the advantage at the time, but it's not winning or gaining some reward that counts in the long run. What matters is that a person is honest and receives the grade he really earns. Deep in his heart he'll know he's done the correct thing and will be a stronger, wiser person for doing so.

The cheater, on the other hand, suffers a guilty conscience. Also he never really understands the material and consequently deprives himself of learning it. And it's just a matter of time before he'll be caught.

MOTIVES BEHIND CHEATING

Your child's question about Tommy provides a good opportunity for you to talk about the reasons why kids cheat. Are they worried that their parents will punish them for not making an A? Are they having learning difficulties but are afraid to admit it? Are they scared that a parent won't love them anymore if they make a low grade?

Posing these questions to your child allows you to emphasize that you'd rather have her be honest with you even if it means giving you disappointing news. Let her know what you would do should she make a low or failing grade, allowing her to see that it wouldn't mean the end of the world or the end of your love for her.

Ask your youngster if she's ever cheated or been tempted to cheat and, if so, under what circumstances. If she has, praise her for being honest with you, acknowledge that she made a mistake and then tell her that mistakes are really lessons. We all make mistakes; the important thing is that we learn from them.

2. SHOULD YOU ALWAYS KEEP A FRIEND'S SECRET?
   How can I tell on him when he's my friend?
   What should I do if a friend steals when I'm in the store with her?

You want your child to know it's important to keep confidences in order to be trusted by friends but that there are times when this general rule doesn't apply. The exceptions are when keeping the secret could hurt someone or where criminal behavior is involved.

To help your youngster understand the exceptions, you'll need to give her some examples: "Jenna, if your friend told you her father was hitting her with a belt until her legs bleed but asked you not to tell anyone, you would owe it to Jenna to tell a responsible adult, such as your parents or your school counselor, so that Jenna could be protected and her father could get help. The adult would know how to go about reporting the problem."

Or, "Honey, if your friend tells you a secret about something that's dangerous—say, he's hiding matches so that he can play with fire— you'd need to tell on him to protect him from the danger he could do to himself as well as other people. Think how you'd feel if you didn't tell and then his house burned down and someone got killed?"

Let your youngster know that a friend's doing drugs would be another appropriate instance to break that friend's confidence. Drugs are both illegal and dangerous, and the child who is taking them can't get help until he's caught.

Help your child realize the difference between gossiping and telling confidences versus telling an adult about something that could be dangerous or hurtful to someone else: "Honey, if your friend tells you she has a crush on a boy in her class and asks you not to tell anyone, you would be violating her confidence and gossiping by telling someone her secret. But if she told you she was so unhappy that she was thinking of killing herself, you would need to break her confidence in order to keep her from hurting herself."

Make it clear that it's important for your child to tell a responsible person about a secret that shouldn't be kept. "If you decide a secret should not be kept, Natalie, don't just go around telling other kids about it. Something that serious needs to be told to an adult who can do something about it. The adult can also help you know whether or not something should be done, just in case you're in doubt."

Let your youngster know you understand how hard it is to tell information that could get a friend in trouble. However, a person has a moral obligation to tell on someone, even a best friend, if that friend is doing something that could be harmful to himself or others. In fact telling can even help the offender.

The example of a child who's offering drugs to peers can help prove your point: "Honey, if you told on a friend who had some marijuana and was selling it to other kids, you'd be helping to make sure those other kids didn't get started on drugs. But you'd also be helping your friend who was selling it, because even though he'd get in trouble, he could then get some help before he became a real drug user."

If your child asks what to do when a friend she's with commits or plans to commit a crime, such as shoplifting, let her know she needs to take a clear stand with her friend. Explain that if she's caught with someone who shoplifts, she's going to be considered guilty right along with her friend. Even if she truthfully explains she did not participate in the act, she'll still be considered an accessory to the crime.

Your youngster could say something like "Melissa, if you're going to steal something, I'm not going to stay in the store with you. You can get into big trouble if you get caught, and I can get into trouble, too, just for being with you." If she discovers that the act has already occurred, your child can tell her friend to return the item immediately. If the friend doesn't respond, tell your youngster she should leave the store but then inform you (or her other parent) about the situation. You can then report the matter to the other child's parent or to the store manager, depending upon the situation.

If your child knows a particular friend shoplifts, suggest she tell the friend, "Amanda, I'm not going to go shopping with you if you steal something. It's wrong to steal, and I don't want to get in trouble if you get caught." Prepare your child for the fact that her friend might take offense and not be willing to continue the friendship, but let her know that sometimes one has to risk losing a friend to stand up for a principle.

3. SHOULD YOU FORGIVE SOMEONE WHEN THEY'VE DONE SOMETHING BAD?
   Shouldn't people be punished when they do bad things?

You'll want your child to know that when you forgive someone, it doesn't mean you agree with what they did. The person might have made a small mistake or a big one, but our goal as human beings is to be able to forgive one another's, and our own, mistakes. We might not approve of the person's behavior, but we can usually still approve of the person.

It might be enough to tell your young child, "Of course you should forgive her, honey. She made a mistake, but we all make them." Or, "Samantha, it's okay to be angry with your sister for locking you in the bathroom, but you can't hold it against her forever. You need to forgive people you love just as they forgive you when you do things you shouldn't do."

An older youngster might be ready for some general philosophy about forgiveness. Part of being a human being is acknowledging that you're not perfect, nor is anyone. Everyone makes mistakes, but mistakes teach us valuable lessons. Although other people's mistakes might make a person understandably bitter or rebellious, those feelings—if they continue—end up hurting the person having them more than the person to whom they're directed.

If you have specific religious views about forgiveness, share them. In most religions forgiveness is a goal. Not forgiving involves setting oneself up as a judge of other people rather than leaving the judging to a Higher Power.

Obviously there are some actions that are so serious and offensive that even a person whose philosophy is to forgive any act will have difficulty doing so. Examples would include murder, physical, or sexual abuse, and tragedies occurring from someone's carelessness or neglect. If something like this has occurred and your child wants to know if the person involved should be forgiven, you might say something like "Terry, I know it's very difficult even to think about forgiving that drunk driver who killed your mother in that car accident. Realize that the man could have been very troubled, confused, or immature and that he will have to live the rest of his life knowing he killed someone. Perhaps one day you will feel forgiveness for him, but I understand that right now that would be a very difficult thing for you to do."

If you are religious, you might wish to add something like "I hope one day you will be able to forgive that man simply because we are taught that only God can judge another person. Our job is to be able to find forgiveness in our hearts no matter how awful a person's actions are, but know that forgiveness in this case is a long process. It's natural you wouldn't feel any forgiveness right now."

If your youngster asks about the need for an offense to be punished, explain to him about various types of punishment. In many cases there are consequences for negative behavior. For example a child who cheats in school might get a zero on his paper if he's caught. Sometimes the worst punishment is one we give ourselves by feeling bad about what we've done. The child who cheated and isn't caught might feel very guilty about what he's done. And of course we have courts that give out punishment for various kinds of crimes, such as robbery and murder. In general the degree of punishment is intended to fit the seriousness of the crime.

When you answer your child's question about the need for punishment, realize she might be asking about it because she wants someone to be punished (such as a brother who treated her unfairly) or is worried that *she* did something wrong and is fearing that some punishment will befall her even though she wasn't caught (for example if she told a lie). Ask her to tell you why she's asking the question, using active listening to determine the source of her concern. If you suspect she's feeling guilty about something she's done (or thought about doing), invite her to confess and get it off her mind.

Reassure your child that not all mistakes necessarily require a punishment. If the person continues to make the same mistake, she'll eventually receive the negative consequence from that behavior. Hopefully the person will learn from the mistake, and no punishment will be necessary.

4. WHY DO WE HAVE TO FOLLOW LAWS?
If you don't get caught, what's so bad about breaking a law?
Why do you drive over the speed limit when it's against the law?

You'll want to teach your child that laws are written to protect the rights and property of every individual. They represent an important guideline for what is considered to be ethically right and wrong. Without them our society would not have a sense of order, and people could behave in ways that are harmful to others (for example, commiting murder) without any penalty.

Give your child a simple example of a law that helps keep order: "Honey, think about what would happen if we did not have a law about driving on the right side of the street. People would be driving up and down both sides, traffic would be jammed up, and there'd probably be a lot more accidents."

Or take a law about stealing: "Sheri, if we had no law about stealing, anyone could walk right into our house and take whatever he wanted. We wouldn't have anything that was really ours to keep, even though we'd paid for it."

An older child can understand the fact that laws can also be changed through an orderly process. If a law seems unfair or inappropriate, people can work within our system to change it. For example women were once paid less than men for doing the same work. Now the law has been changed so that people are paid the same amount regardless of their sex.

If your child asks what's wrong with breaking a law if he's not caught, explain that a person who breaks a law is guilty whether he gets caught or not. Getting away with it doesn't make it right. And the person, knowing he's broken a law, has to deal with his own conscience: "Bernie, even if nobody else knows about something you've done that is against the law, you still know it. You can't hide the truth from yourself. And you can't feel good about yourself when you do things that you know go against your basic beliefs about what's right and what's wrong, even if you get away with them."

Let your youngster know that if he does do something that's against the law, he'll feel better about himself in the long run if he admits his mistake, learns from it, and doesn't repeat it. Even if he's punished, he'll have respect for himself for admitting his error and he won't have to continue living with guilt.

If you're put in the awkward position of having your child point out some behavior of yours that is against the law, such as habitually driving over the speed limit, you'll need to do some soul-searching before you answer. Why do you do it? Do you think the speeding laws are wrong and that therefore you have the right to set your own limit? Do you feel you're a better driver than most folks and have a right to drive faster? Do you think all people speed and only slow down when they know a police car is around? Do you think some laws just don't apply to you?

When you determine your answer, you might decide you don't like it and don't want to answer your child honestly. This discovery in itself can be quite telling and might convince you to change your behavior! In this situation you could consider thanking your child for pointing out your behavior and tell her you intend to change it. You might say, "Helen, I realize I drive over the speed limit a lot. I really shouldn't do that; it's a bad habit I've gotten into. I want to change this, so please tell me if you see me doing it again, okay?"

The point is you are giving your child a double message if you tell him he must obey laws while you break them, whatever the reason. If you break the speed limit, he'll probably follow your example when he begins driving.

5. So What If I Told Leslie I'd Spend the Night? Now I Want to Stay at Mary's. Why Can't I?
   I know I told Jane I'd go to her party tomorrow, but can't I change my mind?

Answering these questions involves teaching your youngster about personal integrity. You want her to understand that the point is not whether or not a person can change her mind but that a person must honor commitments in order to be trustworthy. In the case of social commitments, breaking them at the last minute without a very good reason creates hurt feelings in the person who's been rejected.

You might tell your child, "Amy, you promised Leslie you'd spend the night with her. It would be bad manners to change your mind and stay with Mary, and you would hurt Leslie's feelings. You and Mary can get together another time." Or, "Honey, it's rude to accept an invitation from someone and then cancel it unless you have a very good reason, such as being sick. And it's especially rude to change your mind and go be with somebody else. Think how hurt you'd feel if you were counting on a friend to come over and then found out she'd decided she'd rather be with somebody else!"

In the case of a party, explain that parties have to be planned. The hostess needs to know how many people are coming so that she can have the right amount of food, favors, and so on. If a person who's said she'll come doesn't show up, it leaves the hostess with an empty slot, which could have been filled by someone else: "Erin, what if several girls changed their minds about going to Jane's party? Jane's feelings would be very hurt if she'd planned a nice party and only a few people came."

Let your youngster know that when he makes plans with a friend, he needs to keep his commitment if at all possible. Kids don't like other kids who cancel out at the last minute because a better offer comes along.

6. Is It Wrong to Lie to Keep from Hurting Somebody's Feelings?
   What's a "white lie"?
   What if I don't really lie, but I just don't tell the whole truth? Is that still lying?

Basically you want your child to learn that he should tell the truth. However, there are a few social conventions in which he would seem ill mannered if he were absolutely honest. For example, if his grandmother knitted him a sweater and asked, "Do you like it, honey?" would you really want your child to tell her that he despises aqua mohair cardigans?

So there are times when you might prefer that your child tell a "white lie" to spare hurting someone's feelings. But there are also lies of convenience, which some people call "white lies" because they think the lie isn't really very important. A common example would be telling someone who calls on the phone that a person in the next room isn't home because that person doesn't want to talk to the caller. While you probably think it's okay for your child to tell the first type of "white lie," the lie of convenience really has no justification. So you'll want to explain the difference between the two types of "white lies."

There are times, however, when you want your child to tell the truth even if someone's feelings might get hurt. For instance if you're asking your child to tell you why he's been acting so angry with you all week, you'd want him to tell you that you'd been a super grouch toward him, even though this information might hurt your feelings. When emotional intimacy is at stake, you'll want your youngster to be honest no matter what feelings might result.

So when your youngster asks these kinds of questions, find out what specific situation he's talking about before you answer. If he gives no specific example, you might say, "Well, Josh, it depends on the situation," and go on to give him some examples.

If your child asks if not telling the whole truth is the same as lying, you'll need to explain about lies of omission. Use an example she can relate to, such as "Molly, let's say Danny ran away from home and you knew he was hiding at Stacy's house. Now, if Danny's mom called and asked you if Danny was at Jim's house and you said, 'No, Mrs. Smith, he's not there,' you wouldn't be lying. But if you didn't tell her that Danny was at Stacy's, you'd be withholding important information from her. You'd be implying that you didn't know where Danny was, and that would be the lie. It's not a stated lie, but it's a kind of lie because you are still deceiving Danny's mom." Help your child understand that one can be as deceitful by hiding the truth as by lying deliberately.

7. WHY SHOULD I BE NICE TO HER WHEN SHE'S NOT NICE TO ME? *What's wrong with getting even?*

You might tell your younger child, "Honey, you should always try to be nice to everybody, even if they haven't been nice to you. It makes you a better person." You might also point out that the child who isn't being nice might be unhappy. If your child is a little extra nice, that child might feel happier and consequently act a little nicer himself.

An older child might be less accepting of this simple response, wondering why on earth a person would want to be nice to someone she thinks is mean. This gives you an opportunity to teach her the Golden Rule about treating others the way she would like to be treated. You might also tell her, "Honey, always behave in a way that will make you feel good about yourself deep down inside. This means being friendly, having good manners, being considerate of other people's feelings, and showing you care about people. You don't have to like someone, but you can still treat that person with respect. This will earn you the respect of other people."

If your youngster wants to know what's wrong with getting even, explain the philosophy that two wrongs don't make a right: "Bart, if you try to get even, you just stoop to the same level as the other person. Besides that, it just makes the fighting and bad feelings go on longer. It's much better to continue being your normal self, and eventually everyone will see that other kid for who he is and see you as a forgiving and understanding person."

8. WHY ARE PEOPLE FIGHTING ABOUT ABORTION?
Does an abortion kill a baby?

As with any other moral issue you have firm beliefs about, your answer to these questions will depend on your personal viewpoint. Whether pro-choice or pro-life, you'll want your child to understand that the critical disagreement between the two sides has to do with the question of when a fertilized egg becomes a baby.

You might tell your child something like "Max, some people think a fertilized egg is a baby right from the start and that aborting it is actually murdering a baby. Other people think that the fertilized egg has to go through several stages of growth before it becomes a baby and that destroying those cells early in a woman's pregnancy is not killing a baby. I believe. . . ."

You'll want your child to understand that another important issue in the fight over abortion has to do with the right of a woman to have control over her own body and to make her own moral decision. A person might be against abortion personally but might still be pro-choice because she feels it's unfair to make a law that forces someone to abide by a belief system that person doesn't share.

9. WHY DO SCIENTISTS HAVE TO HURT ANIMALS TO DO MEDICAL
   RESEARCH?
   Don't animals have rights too?

Tell your child that people disagree about whether or not animals
should be used for medical research. The people who think it's necessary think medicine would still be very primitive if research could
not be done on animals. They also point out that people would die
from many diseases had a cure not been found through doing animal
research. This group does not think that animals should be abused
or tortured, however, and they say that there are established laws
that prevent animals from being subjected to cruelty or unnecessary
pain.

The folks on the other side think that most animal research is cruel
since research animals are kept in cages all their lives and are often
subjected to painful operations or procedures that make them sick,
uncomfortable, or cause them to die. These people think that the
gains made in medical research do not make up for the fact that
animals suffer. They feel strongly that animals have rights just as
people do and that humans should not take advantage of animals just
because humans are more powerful than animals are.

Help your youngster realize that these questions are not easy to
answer, and get him to think about the moral dilemma that's involved.
For example, "Honey, think about this: Would you make a rat, a
monkey, a cat, or a dog sick or die in order to possibly find a cure
for a disease that could save a baby's life?"

Such an example can help your child see how difficult it is to solve
some moral dilemmas, even for adults.

MORE SUGGESTIONS

1. Challenge your child's thinking by bringing up moral or ethical
dilemmas for family discussion, perhaps at the dinner table. Examples
might be: "Should parents pay their kids to make good grades?"
"Should moms and dads share equally in housework?" "Should kids
be allowed to swear at home if their parents do?" Listen to your
child's reasoning and then broaden her viewpoint by asking questions
that will cause her to think about issues from "the other side."

2. When your older child watches the news, ask his opinion on
stories that have heavy moral overtones, such as reports of riots and
gang wars. Then share your thoughts with him.

3. Point out examples of integrity and honesty in your child whenever you see them. For example, if she brings you a negative note from her teacher, you might let her know you understand that giving you a note with bad news was a hard thing to do and that not all kids would have done it. This message lets her know you appreciate her honesty.

10
Money/Work

YOU PROBABLY WANT YOUR CHILD TO GENUINELY BELIEVE THAT OLD SAYING, "Money isn't everything!" You don't want her to fall into the keeping-up-with-the-Joneses trap or to grow up equating her self-worth with how much money she makes or has at her disposal.

The way most people get money of course is by working. And the kind of work your youngster ends up doing will probably determine his general lifestyle. While you want your youngster to grow up to do the kind of work that suits his interests and talents, you also hope he'll pick a field that will provide him with enough money to have a financially stable lifestyle that includes a few creature comforts.

In our society the value of a particular kind of work is often equated with the level of income it produces. And power, status, and prestige are often linked with the amount of money a person acquires. As a parent your dilemma becomes how to motivate your youngster to develop a work ethic and strive for a comfortable lifestyle without creating a person who's obsessed with money and materialism.

First you have to get clear about your own values concerning work and money before you'll be comfortable knowing what to tell your child. It's so easy to give the message that money is the key to everything good in life. Television often gives the impression that everybody plays on the beach, parties constantly, has lots of money, and gets immediate gratification of wishes (at least within thirty to sixty minutes!). Yet there are other important values we want to teach our children, including friendship, love, health, service, appreciation of nature and beauty, spirituality, and fun.

To get clear about your own priorities about money, you might ask yourself a number of questions: How do I use my money? Do I like the way I'm spending it? Do I give some of it back through charities, tithing, creating scholarships for education, or contributing to projects that benefit other people or the environment? Do I help my money to grow through savings and investments?

Whatever you do with your money, you're setting a powerful example for your child. Not only will you model for him the way money should be spent, but you'll also be influencing his attitudes about the work he'll probably need to do to earn it.

1. WHY CAN'T WE HAVE A HOUSE AS BIG AS LISA'S?
Why don't you make more money?
Why aren't we rich?

If your family has a steady income, pays the basic bills, and has a measure of financial comfort, your child might think you can afford to buy anything you want. If she has friends who come from more affluent families, she's likely to be unaware of the real differences in your buying power compared with that of her friends' parents.

If she asks why you can't have a bigger home, a swimming pool, a lake house, or whatever, let her know the real reason why you can't or don't. It might be that you simply can't afford it, so you'd tell her truthfully that you think her friend's family either has more money or chooses to put more of the money they have into housing. Or it might be you can afford the item but don't want it. In this case explain your priorities: "Alice, your dad and I decided to build the deck and buy new carpeting for the house instead of getting a pool. We didn't have enough left for a pool too." Or, "Honey, we could afford a bigger house like Lisa's, but we'd rather have our smaller house and be able to take the vacations we all like every year. There's only so much money to go around, and we have to make decisions about the best way we want to spend it."

If she asks why you don't make more money, again reality is the best teacher. Let her know that different jobs carry different kinds of paychecks: "Natalie, I actually make very good money for a teacher. But teachers don't make as much money as people in some of the other professions."

If she's asking because your income has dropped, tell her, "Honey, we're having some tough financial times right now. Our company had to cut everybody's salaries, and I'm lucky even to have a job!" Or, "Stacy, I know it's hard right now because we have less money than we're used to, but since Dad's not working, we all just have to make the best of things. Things happen sometimes that can really change a family's income. It's easy to adjust if you suddenly get a lot more money. But, boy, it's hard when you have to get used to *less!*"

Don't try to protect your child from the reality of your financial situation; at the same time don't frighten him by implying that you might lose your house and belongings. You want him to understand that there is less money, but you don't want to threaten his all-important sense of stability. Simply tell him the facts: Some people have more money and some people have less; sometimes you lose what you've been used to and you have to adjust. Remember that you'll be giving your child a good lesson to follow should he ever experience a similar situation later in life.

If your youngster asks why you're not rich, tell him. If he's young, a simple "Gosh, Tommy, I just don't make enough money to be rich, but we do have enough money to take care of most of the things each of us needs" is likely to satisfy him. With your older child you'll want to give more of an explanation. You might say something like "Rob, being rich has to do with having lots of money through owning a successful business, having a high-salaried job or profession, or inheriting money—and then being able to manage that money in such a way that you make even more money through investments and wise decision making." Again, reassure him that even though you are not rich, there is enough money to take care of him.

Make sure you let your child know that being rich doesn't make a person happy: "Peggy, it might seem like anyone who's rich has it made and will have a very happy life. But it's not how much money you have that determines whether you're happy. In fact many wealthy people are miserable and many poorer folks feel quite happy. We all have to learn to be happy within ourselves, to feel like our lives count for something, and to feel that people we care about also care about us. It's nice to have lots of money, but it's not necessary. Money is just something that can make life easier; it can reduce your worries, but it can't make you happy."

2. TIM'S MOM GOT HIM ONE. WHY WON'T YOU GET ONE FOR ME?
But it's only two dollars! Why can't we buy it?
How come you said you don't have any money? I saw ten dollars in your wallet.

One of the most difficult things to explain to children is the value judgment you make when you decide to buy or not to buy something. If you have the money, your child won't see any reason why you shouldn't buy anything he wants.

When he asks why you won't buy him something one of his friends has, tell him the exact reason. If you don't approve of the item, tell him so and let him know your reason: "Honey, I don't believe in buying a BB gun for an eight-year-old. I think they're too dangerous," or, "Sally, those designer jeans are just too expensive. I'm sorry you're disappointed."

Perhaps you don't want to spend your money on something your child wants because you've already spent your allocated budget on that child or on that item: "Brent, I've already bought your school clothes for this fall, remember?" or, "Honey, I bought you a toy the last time we came shopping; this time it's your brother's turn."

When your child wants something just because another child has it, try to figure out where she's coming from. Is she seeking approval from her peers and does she think that having this particular item will guarantee it? If so, you'll need to tell her that the way to get her peers to like her is to be friendly, not to copy one of them. Or is she just using the example of the other child to try to badger you into getting her what she wants? If this is the case, tell her, "Honey, I don't care if the whole class has one. I told you I'm not buying it for you because...."

Your youngster might think you should grant his request for something simply because it's inexpensive. Explain that the price is not the important point in your denying his request and then tell him what your reason is: "Sammy, I've already bought you two treats today; that's enough for now."

Sometimes you tell your child you don't have enough money for something and he counters by reminding you that he's seen money in your purse or wallet. With a young child you might say, "But that money is for something else, Mark. That's why I don't have the money for you to buy that game today."

You'll need to let an older youngster understand that seeing money doesn't mean that money is there to be spent. You have a household budget with set expenses. You might carry money with you because you plan to use it for a particular purchase. Therefore, in a sense it's already spent: "Mel, that money in my purse is there because I need it for lunch money this week," or, "I know you saw that ten-dollar bill, but I'll be using it later today to pick up the dry cleaning."

To help her understand your financial obligations, tell her about some of the bills you pay each month (your house payment, the phone bill, the amount you need for groceries, etc.). Your child needs to realize that you have financial obligations that you must meet with the money you have available to you.

Remember that you can encourage an older child to earn money of her own by doing chores or by doing jobs for neighbors. That way if she wants designer jeans, she can earn the *difference* between the amount you'd normally spend on jeans and the price of the ones she wants. In addition, you'll be letting her experience both the power and the responsibilities of earning money.

3. DAD, ARE WE RICH?

With this question it's important to figure out what your child is really asking. Does he know a child who's poor and is he afraid that he might have to face similar problems? Does he just want to know if he can have what he wants when he wants it? And what does he mean by "rich"? "Why are you asking this, honey?" or, "What do you think?" are questions you might ask to help you decide how you'll answer.

WHEN CHILD IS CONCERNED THAT HE MIGHT BE POOR

Try to find out why your child thinks you might be poor. Did he overhear a conversation where you were discussing your money worries or talking about your fears of losing your job? Did he hear something on the news that made it sound to him like everyone is going to be poor in the future?

Reassure your youngster, if it's true, that your family is not poor. Tell him you make enough money so that he doesn't have to worry about things like not having food to eat or clothes for school. Then address the reason for his concern by giving him the factual information he needs.

WHEN CHILD WANTS YOU TO BUY HIM SOMETHING

Explain to your youngster that just because you have the money for something doesn't mean you're just going to give him anything he desires: "We have enough money to live comfortably, Chuck, but that doesn't mean we can be reckless about the way we spend it." Or, "Well, Hank, I can afford to buy you that remote-control car, but being able to buy it isn't the only thing to consider. It's quite expensive, and I'd rather you earn some of the money before we buy it. Your working for part of it will convince me that you really want that car. And I also think you would feel very good about yourself if you helped earn it."

CHILD IS ATTEMPTING TO DEFINE "RICH"

If your child is young, you could define "being rich" for her by saying, "Lacey, we really don't make enough money to call ourselves rich!" or, "Honey, sometimes I feel like we're rich because we have enough money to buy most of the things we want. Perhaps another person who has more money woudn't think we were rich."

With your older youngster you'll have to get into the relativity of wealth. One easy way might be to say something like "Holly, our family has a lot more money than some families, so I'm sure that those families would consider us rich. But we don't have anywhere near the money other families have, so those other families probably wouldn't think we were rich at all!" Or you could make the point by saying something like "Honey, we consider those people who live in the projects and have no jobs to be poor, but if we lived in Bangladesh, where people live in the streets with no homes and very little food, we'd think the people in the projects weren't quite so poor."

Another pragmatic definition of being "rich" is when a person has enough money to have a *choice* about working or not working. A person might choose not to work because she has lots of money, or she might be satisfied with less money and live a less expensive lifestyle.

Point out that a person never really knows just how much money another person has by the amount of money that person spends. Some very wealthy people spend very little; many people who aren't wealthy overspend and are in financial trouble because of it!

Use this question about being rich as an opportunity to point out to your youngster that there are many kinds of riches. A person might not have much money, but she could be rich in friendships, accomplishments, talents, having loving people in her life, and her ability to live a joyful life.

4. WHY IS JOHNNY POOR?
   How come I get to have lots of money and he doesn't?
   Should I give him some of my money?
   Can't we pay for him to go to camp with me?

When your young child notices the discrepancy between his life-style and that of another child, simply explain, "That little boy's family doesn't have as much money as we have, David." Let an older youngster know that many factors operate to make someone poor. The child he's asking about might have parents who aren't working, or a parent might work but make very little money because he works a minimum-wage job. Perhaps the child's family has a steady income but there are many children to support, or maybe someone in the family is ill and there are high medical expenses to pay off.

Help your child realize that there are many different circumstances that can lead to a person's being poor. Then make sure he understands that a lack of money doesn't say anything about that person's character, intelligence, or value as a human being.

When your child asks if she can give a poor child some of her money, let her know you're pleased at her generosity. Then tell her there might be occasions when she might buy the child something requiring a small amount of money (such as a candy or ice-cream treat). However, caution her that if she constantly bought things for another child, the other child could feel very embarrassed. It doesn't feel good to accept gifts from others when you can't reciprocate the favor: "Honey, if your friend Sally was always buying you treats and you never had any money to spend on her, wouldn't you feel embarrassed about it? You'd feel like you weren't being a very good friend to her since you couldn't give her something back at least some of the time. Well, that's why you wouldn't want to give money to Melissa constantly, because she doesn't have any money and she'd end up feeling bad that she couldn't return the favor."

If your child asks you to pay for something fairly expensive for a child who can't afford to pay himself, such as summer camp, your answer would depend upon your financial circumstances. If you could easily afford it, and if it was acceptable to that child's parents, you might decide to pay for the other child, especially if the other youngster is one of your child's good friends. If it's not within your budget, just tell him so: "Honey, I'd like to be able to pay for Josh to go to camp with you, but I just don't have the money for it."

Whenever you're giving to a particular child or family, the point you want to make about this kind of giving is that it should be an unusual circumstance rather than an everyday event. If it's done more frequently, you set the other person up to feel embarrassed or obligated. However, you can give money to charities, churches, or other organizations or become an anonymous donor to a particular child or family. There are ways to give to poor people, whether it's clothing or camp, which don't result in feelings of embarrassment or obligation on the part of the recipient. A person can also give of their time rather than their money. Volunteering to work on a community project or to donate time to a nursing home, hospital, or shelter are also ways to help the poor.

5. **But I Used Up All My Allowance! Won't You Buy It for Me?**
   Can I have some of my next week's allowance now? I'll pay you back.

Allowances are great because they give you the opportunity to teach your child real-life money management. The problem is you might end up teaching him the road to financial disaster if you allow him to wheedle his way around your better judgment!

When your child tells you his allowance is used up and asks you to foot the bill for something he wants, you might decide to honor his request the first time, pointing out how he got himself into this predicament and suggesting what he could have done differently. If he doesn't learn his lesson, however, it's better to deny his second request. Otherwise you teach him that he doesn't really have to stick to his allowance because you'll be there to cover for him. Even if he blows all of his lunch money a second time, it's better to let him make himself a lunch to take to school than to continue funding his irresponsible behavior.

When your child asks for an advance on next week's allowance with promises to repay you or to have you deduct the amount from the next week's funds, you might want to give him this opportunity. If he follows through on his own, you can praise him for being so responsible.

What typically happens, though, is that you either forget he owes you money or you decide to write off the bad debt. While magnanimous and well intended, you've then set yourself up for the same thing to happen all over again! Instead you might tell him, "Mike, the last time you borrowed allowance from me in advance, you got really angry with me when I asked you to keep your part of the bargain and repay me. I don't want to go through something like that again. Try me again in a few months and we'll see if by then you've learned to remember to pay back your debts."

6. **Mom, My Teacher Told Us About This Wonderful Science Camp. Can I Go?**
   Will you have the money to pay for my college?

If you've easily got the money, neither of these questions will tug at your heartstrings. But if you don't, or if you're not sure you can swing it financially, you might feel quite guilty. After all, parents are programmed that they should sacrifice for their children and provide them with every opportunity for educational enrichment and for the development of their talents. You might be tempted to go to great lengths to try to provide the money, working two jobs or making all kinds of personal sacrifices. But there's no need for this; your job as a parent is to provide love, support, acceptance, and guidance and the basic physical necessities for your child. Expensive extras—even college in this era of soaring tuitions—are luxuries, not necessities.

So be realistic. If you don't have the funds, be up front with your child about it: "Damon, I'd love for you to be able to go to that camp, but Dad and I just don't have the money for it. I'm sorry, honey." If the funds for camp are within your child's earning capacity (or perhaps you could match funds with him), suggest he plan to go the following year and work toward making that happen. Even elementary school children can find ways to earn or save money, and your youngster will feel good about earning his own way.

If she's asking about college and you see no way that you'll be able to afford it, you might say, "Rosemary, right now I don't see how we'll have enough money to pay for college expenses. We'll certainly help you if we can, but I don't want you counting on it. However, many kids go to college without their parents' help. There are scholarships and loans available, and you can also work to earn your own way. Anyone who really wants to can find a way to go, and we'll help you explore all the avenues, including helping you with finances if we can."

7. How Will I Know What to Be When I Grow Up?
   Since we have lots of money, why would I ever have to work? What if I don't like my job?

These kinds of questions give you a wonderful opportunity to discuss your values about work and its place in a person's life. After all, a job can be something a person does to make money so that she can do what she really wants to do when she gets off work. The work might or might not be personally satisfying, but it provides a means to an end. Or a job can bring meaning to a person's life by being something she enjoys, something that makes her feel good about herself, and perhaps something that makes her feel that she's contributing to the good of other people.

You probably hope your child will find interesting, meaningful work suited to her talents and capabilities. She might or might not make a lot of money doing this, but it's unlikely you'd advise her to enter a line of work solely for the purpose of making money. The saying "Do what you love and love what you do" makes good psychological sense.

So you might tell your young child, "Angela, right now you don't have to figure out what you want to be when you grow up; you'll have lots of time to decide." With an older child you could add, "Honey, you might even change your mind a bunch of times, even after you've grown up. Even adults change careers when they find something new that they want to do. The important thing is that you enjoy your work and that it makes you feel good about yourself."

Let her know, however, that she probably won't be doing exactly what she loves with her first job: "Honey, you might have to work at something you're not thrilled with for a while, either because you need the money or because you have to use a job as a stepping-stone to get the job you really want. But if you keep your goal in mind, use common sense, pay attention to your feelings, and stick with what you believe in, you'll probably get where you want to go."

If your child wants to know why he would have to have a job when you have plenty of money to support him, let him know that working is a normal step in life and that most people work. The more important point is that a person feels better about himself when he earns what he has rather than having it all given to him and that work brings with it a great sense of personal satisfaction: "Jody, if I just gave you all the money you ever needed or wanted when you grow up and you never had to do any kind of work, you wouldn't end up feeling good about yourself. It might sound like fun now, never to have to do any work and just play the days away having fun, but that type of life would soon become very boring. We all need to feel we're accomplishing something in order to feel good about ourselves and our lives. If we just supported you all of your life, we'd be treating you as if you were someone who couldn't take care of herself; that would be a real put-down!"

If your youngster asks what would happen if he ended up doing work he doesn't like, let him know that it's okay to change to something different. In fact he might need to experiment with several types of jobs before he figures out exactly what he likes best. While there are times when a person has to stay in a job he doesn't like for a while, he can wait for or create an opportunity to do something he enjoys. In the meantime he can make the best of the job he's in until he has a chance to change it.

8. Jeannie's Mom Stays Home All Day. Why Can't You?
I don't want to go to day care. Why can't you stay home with me after school?

In these days of two-career and single-parent households, mothers staying at home seem to be more the exception than the rule. But some moms don't work, and your child might envy the one whose mother is home after school, who volunteers in her child's classroom, and who can transport her child to lessons and other after-school activities.

When your child asks these questions, it's tempting to get defensive and rush in to explain your point of view. However, you might first check to see why your child is asking you about this. Is something going on in her after-school care that is negative or frightening?

Once you begin explaining why you don't stay home, you'll probably have one of two answers. First, you might not have any option: "Honey, I have to work in order to make our family's expenses. Besides, my working allows us to have some extras—like vacations, a nicer home, more recreation, more clothing, and so on—that we wouldn't be able to have if we just had your dad's income."

Second, you might be in a position where you *could* stay at home but you choose not to because your work brings you personal satisfaction: "Honey, it's very important to me to be able to work *and* to have a family. I'm not the kind of mom who would be happy staying home all day" or, "Melinda, my career makes me feel very good about myself. I really enjoy my work, and it gives me a lot of personal satisfaction. Both my family and my work are very important to me."

Acknowledge to your child that there are some advantages to having a mom who doesn't work, but there are also advantages to having a mom who does. Reassure her that you will always make sure you and she have time together and that you will make every effort to be there for her whenever she needs you. Let her know that even though you aren't at her school during the day, you still help her school by contributing baked goods, doing phone work, going to PTA meetings, helping with special projects, and so on.

If you are a mother, you might feel a pang of guilt when your child lets you know he'd prefer you to stay home and not work. Remember that a mother's staying home with her child is no guarantee that the mother-child interaction is positive. On the other hand many working mothers find creative ways to have quality time with their children. In other words if you have personal qualities that make you a good parent, you'll demonstrate those qualities whether you work or not.

9. IF MOMMY HATES HER JOB, WHY DOESN'T SHE QUIT?
Why do you always say work is hard?
How come some people like their work and some don't?
Is Mommy working just because of me?

If your young child asks why you don't quit a job you dislike, you could say something like "Because we need the money, Neil. I don't want to quit unless I find another job I like better." If he's old enough for a minilesson in economics, tell him, "Honey, it's not always that easy to find another job. Sometimes you have to settle for something you don't like because there isn't a better job available where you live. Rather than have to move, you'd prefer just to put up with the job you have a little longer. If you just quit working, then you're not going to be getting any money and you won't be able to pay your bills."

If your youngster wants to know why you say your work is hard, use the analogy between your going to work and your child's going to school. Even if a person basically likes school, there are good days and not-so-good days. A person needs to think about the good things and just keep on going.

If he asks why some people like their work and some don't, let him know that being happy with your job means finding a good match between your personality, interests, and talents and the kind of work you're doing. It also means feeling you are paid fairly and that you're not feeling your boss or company is taking advantage of you. Many people get stuck in jobs they don't like because they have no other choice at the moment; they need the money.

If your child asks if you are working just because of her, chances are she's feeling guilty. She might have overheard you talking about working to be able to afford more opportunities for her and/or her siblings, or you might have told her directly that you're working to provide her with a better lifestyle. If you seem overworked or complain frequently about your work, she could feel responsible for your dissatisfaction.

Take the burden off her by saying something like "Honey, I do work because I want to be able to give you a better life than what you would have if I didn't make that money. But I'm also working for all of us. I get to have more things I want, too, and our whole family gets to do things—like go on vacations—that we couldn't do as often if I didn't work."

Even if you're having a difficult time with your job, remember that what you say about working can influence your child's thinking on the subject. Point out the positives as well as the negatives; you don't want to give the overall impression that work is something to be dreaded.

10. WHY DID DADDY GET FIRED? DID HE DO SOMETHING WRONG?
    If people work hard, don't they get to keep their jobs?
    So how come Daddy doesn't just start another job now?

When your child asks why a parent was fired, tell her the truth without putting that parent down. "Nicole, your dad and his boss have been seeing things differently for some time now. The boss finally decided he didn't want Dad working there anymore."

Sometimes a parent is fired because of a personal problem that is obvious to the child. If this is the case, acknowledge the problem matter-of-factly: "Mike, you know your dad has been having lots of problems lately. He's been missing work a lot because he hasn't been feeling well (has been drinking a lot, has been having trouble controlling his temper, etc.)."

You might tell your youngster, if it's true, that Dad wasn't really right for that particular job and that he's learned he would be better doing a different kind of work. Let your child know that many people work in a certain type of job or career for a time and then realize their personality or talents are more suited to a different line of work. This explanation teaches that all of us have strengths and weaknesses and that not doing well in one type of job can be seen as a lesson rather than a failure.

Whatever the reason Dad lost his job, remind your child to be supportive: "Honey, your dad feels bad about losing his job. We all need to help him by doing what we can to help him feel better. That means not complaining about not having as much money right now, helping out with chores so that Dad doesn't have to worry about them, and letting him know we all love him."

Your child might ask why a person who's hardworking could lose his job. Explain that working hard is something employers want but that this in itself gives no guarantee of job security. People can lose their jobs because they disagree with the folks who are in power, because someone comes along who can do a better job, because the person behaves in a way that the boss or coworkers don't like, be-cause the boss wants to make a change, or because the business is in financial trouble itself and must cut back on employees: "Charlie, your job isn't what gives you security. Your security lies within you, in your abilities, your talents, and your accomplishments. Nobody can take those things away from you."

If your child wants to know why a parent who's fired just doesn't run right out and find another job, let him know that finding the right job takes time, sometimes months. And if a person is specialized or highly qualified, he's likely to have more trouble getting a job that matches his abilities and potential: "Arnie, Dad is very good at his work and he's done it a long time. Sure, he could go out and find just any old job that wouldn't pay much, but with his training and experience he can find a better job he really likes that will pay the kind of money he's been used to making, maybe even more. Dad wants to give himself some time to find the right job, and we need to let him know we're behind him all the way."

MORE SUGGESTIONS

1. Assign your youngster some regular household chores that are appropriate to her age. Even a young child can take her dirty dishes from the table to the sink and can pick up her toys and put them away. An older youngster can have responsibilities, such as loading and unloading the dishwasher, feeding a pet, making his bed, cleaning his room, and so forth. Having to do chores develops responsibility in your child and helps give him the message that everyone in a family contributes some type of useful "work."

2. To help your child learn how a business operates, let him experiment with a minibusiness, such as a lemonade stand. But don't just make the lemonade, put it out on a table in the yard, and tell him to sell it. Show him "the business end" of this venture. Help him figure out his expenses (cost of lemonade, paper cups, your labor in making the drink and setting up the stand, etc.), his total retail sales (money collected), and his actual profit. While you might decide to pay his expenses and let him keep all the money he earns, the point is to let him first see what's involved in running a business.

3. When your child starts speculating about the kind of job he wants to have when he grows up, encourage him to ask some adults about their work and what they do and don't like about it. For example, if she thinks she wants to be a pediatrician, suggest she talk to one about what's involved in a career in medicine.

11
Habits/Addictions

WE ALL KNOW PEOPLE WHO ARE INTELLIGENT AND RATIONAL, YET WHO CONtinue to pursue some behavior that puts their health, self-esteem, and personal relationships at risk. Why people do things that are bad for them is the core question to be asked about all sorts of harmful habits and addictions.

As a parent, your concern is that your youngster not get caught up in any negative behavior pattern. You don't want him to develop a dependence on cigarettes, alcohol, prescribed or illicit drugs, too much food, or anything else that hooks him into some form of self-destruction.

Since prevention makes a cure unnecessary, you'll want to begin talking with your child about issues such as smoking, drinking, and drug use when he's in elementary school. Preaching, threatening, or becoming highly emotional won't work. But matter-of-fact, informative dialogues during which you take your child's questions seriously, get his input as well as giving your opinions, and listen openly can give you a wonderful chance to influence his thinking about these matters.

Of course things get complicated if you have a problem in one of these areas yourself. If you smoke, for example, you'll be trying to convince your child about the folly of doing something you yourself are doing. If you're in this awkward position, use it to your advantage. Tell your child how and why you think you developed your habit and be up front about the fact you're telling him about it because you want him to learn from your mistakes.

1. WHAT'S AN ADDICT?
   Can addictions ever be cured?
   Am I going to get addicted to my allergy medicine?

When your young child asks about the word *addict* or *addiction*, simply explain, "Marsha, an addict is a person who takes drugs or alcohol and can't stop" or, "We say that a person has an addiction to drugs or alcohol if she can't stop herself from taking them."

With your older youngster you'll want to go into the broader meaning of addiction: "Honey, an addiction means that a person can't stop some behavior, whether it's using drugs, smoking, gambling, drinking, or any other activity that has a bad effect on him. Sometimes the addiction is physical: The person's body gets so hooked on a substance—cocaine for example—that the person will become physically ill if he can't get it. Many addictions, however, are psychological; even if the person's body doesn't actually need the substance, the person has gotten so emotionally dependent on it that he feels desperate if he doesn't have it and he'll do almost anything to get it."

If your child asks if addictions can be cured, let him know that they usually can if the person is sincerely dedicated to stopping the addictive behavior. However, curing an addiction is very difficult work and often requires the help of a professionally trained counselor.

If your child wonders about becoming addicted to her allergy medicine or to some other medication she takes, it's time to explain the difference between illicit drugs and prescribed medicines. Many illicit drugs are physiologically addicting; some prescription drugs are, too, if a person takes too much of them for too long a time. This is one of the reasons why doctors give prescriptions that tell patients exactly how much medicine to take and for how long, so that they can't get addicted to an addicting medicine if they follow the doctor's orders.

However, many prescription drugs aren't addicting even if a person takes them for a long period of time. Medicines given to children, such as those prescribed for allergies, are not addicting and can be taken over a long time period.

2. WHY CAN'T YOU QUIT SMOKING, MOMMY?
   Why do people smoke when it's bad for them?
   How can we get Dad to stop smoking?

With all the education in the schools about the harmful effects of smoking, you can be sure your child is going to ask you to explain yourself if you have this habit. When he asks why you can't quit, you'll need to explain that quitting smoking can be very difficult. Many grown-ups feel helpless about quitting and might even choose not to try to quit, even though they know smoking is bad for them. Then tell your youngster why you think you smoke. Probably the most common reason is that many people smoke to relieve tension. It's kind of the adult version of a kid's sucking her thumb, swinging her leg, twiddling her hair, or biting her nails.

"But how can you smoke when it's bad for you?" might be his next question. Acknowledge that you know smoking is very bad for your health and that you feel very frustrated with yourself for not being able to break this habit. Then turn the conversation into a lesson, pointing out the wisdom of never starting to experiment with smoking in the first place. "Honey, I wish that when I was your age, I had really understood how hard this habit is to break and how bad smoking is for you. I never would have started."

If your child begins a campaign to get you or the other parent to quit smoking, let him know you appreciate his good intentions. But make it clear that each person has the responsibility for his own choices; a child is not responsible for a parent's health. However, you might encourage him to talk to the other parent about his concerns (perhaps even asking that parent to quit) and then leave the issue alone: "Justin, it's not kind to constantly bug someone about a habit that the person probably feels bad enough about already."

Let your child know about the peer pressure she might face about smoking when she becomes a teenager. Explain that many teens experiment with cigarettes because it makes them feel grown up and because they think smoking is "cool." Tell her it's the kids who *don't* experiment with getting addicted to cigarettes who are the more mature ones.

Because of the recent evidence of the harmful effects of *passive* smoking, consider smoking (if you do) outside the house or in a designated area inside the house. This will give your child another message that you care about his health and reinforce the fact that you consider smoking to be a negative practice.

3. WHY DOES DADDY DRINK SO MUCH?
   Daddy scares me when he's drunk. Can't you get him to stop drinking?
   When is somebody who drinks an alcoholic?
   You and Mommy drink. Why can't I?

Tell your child that most people who drink too much are using alcohol to cover up their feelings. They might be sad, angry, or frightened but don't want to feel these painful feelings, so they drink too much. Or they might be very shy around people and drink in order to feel more relaxed. The alcohol numbs them emotionally, distracting them and making them feel a little better at first. However, the feelings that caused them to drink in the first place don't go away by being ignored. They come back, the person drinks again, and the cycle is repeated.

After giving the general explanation, be more specific about the possible reasons why the person drinks excessively: "Honey, Daddy has been upset since Grandmother died last year. I think that might be why he is drinking so much lately." Or, "Your dad is under a lot of stress with his job right now, Marty. Your dad loves us, but he's going through a real tough time right now." Be sure to add that although the reason for drinking might be understandable, the drinking will never solve the problem or resolve the feelings.

If your child asks at what point a person who drinks becomes an alcoholic, tell her it's when a person regularly loses control of his behavior when he drinks. Some examples are: He can't stop drinking once he starts; he does things he wouldn't normally do, such as losing control of his temper; he can't remember what went on while he was drinking; his drinking keeps him from normal activities, such as going to work.

Let your youngster know that a person who's an alcoholic is usually the last person to admit he has a problem, because he's in a state of denial. Friends and loved ones can point out to him the negative effects of his drinking, but he convinces himself they are wrong and makes excuses for his behavior.

If someone in your family abuses alcohol and behaves in a manner that frightens your child, she might ask you why you can't stop that person from drinking. Even though you'll be clear that you can't "make" a person do or not do anything, realize that your youngster needs to feel there's an adult in the house who will protect her. When a parent's behavior while drinking is frightening to a child, be honest with her and admit the problem. Let her know that you'll seek help for the family from a specially trained counselor or from a support group, even if the person who abuses alcohol refuses to participate.

If your child points out that you drink and asks why she can't, tell her that drinking alcohol is against the law until a person reaches a certain age. For an analogy she might relate to, ask her why she thinks children aren't allowed to drive. As you discuss this with her, you'll eventually get around to the fact that children would be too impulsive and would drive recklessly. Point out that the same issues of carelessness and impulsivity are involved in the drinking issue.

Let your child know that a person who drinks needs to be able to drink responsibly, since alcohol can be addicting and can be dangerous. For example many automobile accidents are caused by people who were driving while under the influence of alcohol.

If you use wine for religious occasions or special family holidays and choose to let your child have a small amount on those occasions, let your youngster know that this form of alcohol use is different from recreational drinking. The quantity of alcohol is limited, and the act of drinking alcohol is symbolic, not an end in itself.

4. WHY DOES DADDY ACT SILLY WHEN HE DRINKS BEER? *Why does Mom yell so much when she drinks?*

Your child will notice any obvious behavior changes that occur in anyone who's drinking alcohol, and it's not uncommon for folks who drink recreationally to be less inhibited or to act a little silly when they drink. Let your youngster know that many people drink when they want to relax or celebrate because alcohol does have the effect of "loosening them up." However, caution your child that there's a big difference between getting a little less inhibited while drinking and getting out of control due to overdrinking. Let her know, too, that a little alcohol can make a person feel good, but too much alcohol (and that amount varies from person to person) will actually make a person depressed.

If your child asks why Mom yells so much when she's been drinking, explain that alcohol makes people less inhibited about any feeling they're having, not just happy feelings. If a person is angry when she drinks, even though she might not realize she's angry, her true feelings will come out if she has too much alcohol: "Honey, it's not that drinking too much turns you into a different person; it's that drinking too much can bring out feelings you might have hiding inside you."

Regarding his question about his mother's behavior, you might say something like "Joe, I'll talk to your mom about her yelling when she drinks. You can tell her how you feel about it too. Mom might not realize that she does this and how it makes us feel, so I think she should know." If the situation continues, seek help from a mental-health professional.

5. WHY DO PEOPLE TAKE DRUGS?
Why can't I try a drug just once to see what it feels like?
Mommy takes pills all the time. Is she addicted?
If pot is illegal, why do you and Dad do it?

Tell your child that many teenagers begin to take drugs because of pressure from their peers. They think it's fun to experiment, they think nothing bad can happen to them since they've seen their friends take the drug with no bad effects, and they are curious about the "high" feeling they've heard drug users talk about.

Let your youngster know that kids who get addicted to drugs are often searching for a feeling of happiness or joy that they're unable to get in their lives. The drug might help them *temporarily* escape loneliness, anxiety, or depression by making them forget their problems. The trouble is those feelings don't go away. In fact they can get worse as the kid moves farther into the world of drugs.

Make sure your child knows that there are many drug-free ways to get "high" on life: "Angie, it's a great feeling to achieve something you've worked for, to perform your best in a sport, to do something nice for someone else, to share happy moments with a friend. Drugs are a fake way to feel good, and even that doesn't last very long. When the drug wears off, the same old problems are still there."

Your child might want to know what would be wrong with trying a drug just one time to see how it feels. Tell her that nobody starts out taking a drug thinking he'll get hooked on it, yet they end up with an addiction. Everyone starts out thinking, "I'll just do this once or a few times to see what it's like." Of course if he takes it once and it feels good, why not do it again? He'll begin to do it a little more often, telling himself he can quit anytime. Then all of a sudden he's become addicted. There's just no way of knowing in advance who will and who won't develop an addiction.

Also, let your youngster know that not all people feel great when they take a drug the first time. Sometimes they react very badly and have a frightening experience: "There's just no way to know in advance if you'll be one of the people who might have an awful experience the very first time, no matter how many of your friends got a good feeling from the drug."

If your child asks about the other parent's being addicted to pills, your answer will depend on whether or not this is true. If Mom is taking pills as prescribed by a doctor, reassure him that she's not addicted and is doing what she's supposed to do with her medication. If she's misusing prescription drugs in an addictive way, tell your child the truth and let him know what you're doing or she's doing to get help with this problem. It's important to admit a parent's addiction when a child asks about it so that the youngster will learn the importance of trusting his own instincts in protecting himself.

If you use an illicit drug, such as marijuana, and your child finds out about it, realize your child has, in effect, been given your permission to use drugs when he's older no matter what you say to him about this. Perhaps you think an adult should have the right to use such drugs if he chooses and that the laws about drug use should be changed. If this is the case, explain this philosophical position to your child, but make it clear that your stance is controversial and that your behavior is illegal. Tell him you would not want him to make the same choice until he's an adult. Just as he can't drive or drink until he is of a certain age, be clear that you don't want him engaging in the dangerous behavior of using drugs until he's an adult, no matter what he might decide at that time.

6. Why Do You Say Bad Words But You Won't Let Me Say Them?
   Why does Dad swear so much?
   Why is cursing bad?

Tell your child that, right or wrong, there are certain standards of behavior for adults that are different for children. Swearing is one of those behaviors that is often considered acceptable for adults.

Let him know that kids get into trouble when they're overheard swearing. If they're in school, they'll get some negative consequence, perhaps going to the principal's office. If they're heard swearing in a friend's home, the adults who live there might not invite them back. Even adults have to use discretion about when and where they swear, and there are adults who don't appreciate swearing in any circumstance.

If your youngster asks why Mom or Dad swears so much, explain the swearing as a bad habit: "Elaine, sometimes we all get into habits. Your dad has many fine qualities, but one of his weaknesses is that he swears a lot. If he swears in front of you, don't take it personally, honey; it's just something Dad does when he loses his temper."

Even if your child accepts that adults can swear and kids aren't supposed to, she still might want to know what's so bad about swearing in the first place. Tell her that nobody ever improved her vocabulary by swearing; it's much better to find other words to express frustration when we're upset, since even when we grow up, we might be somewhere where swearing is inappropriate. Many people also object to swearing that includes a reference to God or other religious figures. Teach your youngster that it's never okay to use swear words that denigrate a religious, racial, or other special group.

7. WHY DON'T YOU WANT DAD TO GO TO THE RACETRACK?
   What's a compulsive gambler?
   Aren't people who gamble afraid they'll lose all their money?
   How can Daddy gamble away our money if he loves us?

If a parent gambles foolishly, to the point where the family income is compromised, a child will quickly pick up on the tension between the parents. If this happens in your household and your youngster asks why you are upset that the other parent goes to the racetrack (or buys lottery tickets, plays the casinos, etc.), tell your young child something simple like "Mark, Dad and I disagree about betting money on horses (games, etc.)."

You can give your older child more detail about the problems people can have when they gamble: "Honey, more people lose than win in gambling; otherwise the racetracks, lotteries, and casinos would go out of business. Sometimes people get so caught up in the hope of winning that they lose their common sense and keep betting even though they don't have the money for it. They think the next bet will be the one that will make them rich, so they keep spending more money. Pretty soon they get desperate because they've lost so much money, so they spend even more money trying to win back what they've spent. It's a vicious circle. The reason I don't like Dad going to the track is because I think he spends too much money gambling."

Let your child know that many people gamble for entertainment and do not develop any problem with it. However, a compulsive gambler is someone who has gotten out of control, spending money needed for other expenses on betting and even borrowing money in order to continue gambling. Such a person eventually stops feeling good about himself because of all the money he's wasted, and then he becomes very depressed because of the debt he's created.

If your child asks why someone would gamble when he knows he might lose money, tell her gamblers are taking the chance because they know it's *possible* to win. The idea the next bet will make one rich is a very powerful and exciting temptation.

Let your child know that some people don't believe in gambling of any sort because of the harm it can do. Other folks feel it's fun to gamble so long as a person determines ahead of time how much money he's willing to lose and then quits gambling if he loses that amount. The problem of course is that a person can intend to quit when he loses, but he might not follow through on his commitment to himself.

If gambling is an issue in your household because someone is an out-of-control gambler, your youngster might ask how that person can continue losing the family money if he loves his family. Let her know that compulsive gambling, like any other addiction, has nothing to do with the amount of love a person has for his family. Even the most loving people can have personal weaknesses and problems.

8. WHY IS THAT PERSON SO FAT?
   How come Sally says she's so fat even though she's skinny?
   I saw Tom's mom sit down and eat half a cake, a big container of ice cream, and then a bag of cookies! How could she have done that?

When your child asks why people get fat, the simple answer is that they eat more calories than they burn. Of course it's a whole lot more complicated than that, because two people can eat the same amount of food and one person's body will burn up the calories while the other person's body won't. Each of us has our own rate of burning calories, and the best way to burn more calories is to exercise.

Besides this, some people are much more concerned with food than others. For most people who have no problem with weight, food is there to provide nourishment. But for many folks, eating favorite foods is a way of comforting themselves and feeling good. Most people who get fat simply enjoy eating, although some scientists think there might be some mechanisms in a person's brain chemistry that cause a person to eat more food than his body requires for hunger.

Be sure you let your child know that normal bodies come in a variety of shapes and sizes and that our society is far too concerned with thinness. Although television advertising implies that everyone must be thin to be successful or happy, this simply is not true. Our society has made such an issue of our figures and physiques that we see people becoming obsessed with weight. The truth is that being excessively thin is quite unattractive and that a person needs to find an appropriate weight for herself that is comfortable and physically healthy.

An older child might pick up on the fact that many people, especially teenage girls, become preoccupied with their weight and might think they're fat when they're really thin. Tell your child that an extremely thin person who think's she's fat might have an emotional illness called anorexia. A person with this illness might starve herself because she thinks she's fat or is desperately afraid she'll gain weight. If a person with this illness doesn't receive professional help, she can cause much physical damage to her body and even, in severe cases, die.

If your child asks how someone who's not obese can binge on food, explain that the person might get rid of the food after the binge by making herself throw up. Let her know this behavior is very dangerous and that people who do it regularly can end up with many medical problems that can also, in serious cases, cause death. A person who binges and vomits (or takes laxatives) to control her weight usually feels very guilty about this behavior, but finds herself addicted to doing it until she seeks professional help.

MORE SUGGESTIONS

1. Most children are being exposed to drug education programs in elementary school. Help your youngster absorb this information by showing interest and asking your child to share the materials with you. If your community doesn't have such a program, talk to your PTA or church about starting one.

2. For a fun way to break a child's habit of saying words you don't approve of, put an amount of nickels or dimes in a jar and remove one every time the child says the word. At the end of a week the child gets to keep what's left in his jar!

3. Teach your child about good nutrition in a casual manner as you grocery-shop. Be sure to provide a variety of snacks that are low in fat and/or high in fiber. Don't battle over food or make it a reward (or penalty), as this can set up a power struggle over food.

12
The Environment

As a parent today, you might feel ill prepared to talk to your child about a topic your parents might not have thought about, much less discussed with you. While it's always been true, humanity is becoming much more aware that everything existing on the planet is interdependent. All of the kingdoms—minerals, plants, animals, and humans—have to exist in balance in order for living things to have the air, water, and food that are necessary for life. Because our planet's survival is at stake, you'll need to raise your child's consciousness about environmental concerns.

You might feel a little awkward in this area because you are also learning about environmental issues. Thanks to the media, we're all becoming much more aware of the survival issues facing future generations. Fortunately education about the environment is being put into our elementary school curriculums, and children are being taught what they and their families can do to make a difference.

Realize, however, that your child might become frightened by some of the information he'll be getting. After all, when he hears about all the pollution of air, food, and water, he just might get scared to breathe, eat, or drink! Add to that some talk about our planet burning up, either from the sun or from a nuclear holocaust, and your youngster might quite understandably begin to worry if the Earth will still be here if he's lucky enough to survive until adulthood!

Your job, then, is to walk the tricky line of impressing him with the seriousness of environmental issues without scaring him into a state of insecurity and depression. Fortunately the message of environmentalists is that we *can* do something about the situation of our planet *if* we begin *now* to reverse the damage that's been done.

Probably the biggest difficulty in helping your child understand environmental problems is the same thing that's made it difficult for adults: We don't see the immediate effects of harmful environmental practices. It's only through education rather than direct experience that most of us come to understand the serious consequences of what might seem like an insignificant action.

You can help greatly in this process by discussing environmental issues in your home and by actively taking steps to be environmentally user-friendly. Look to your child as a coteacher in this area and enjoy learning together about the issues.

1. I JUST DROPPED ONE SODA CAN. WHAT'S THE BIG DEAL?
   Why can't I throw the Styrofoam cup in the lake?
   If Billy throws a gum wrapper or his lunch sack on the ground, what should I do?

When your child asks about throwing away soda cans, tell her that these cans, as well as other aluminum products (such as cat food cans, aluminum foil, TV dinner trays, etc.) can be reused. They can go to factories that melt them down in chips, mold them into solid aluminum bars, and then roll them into sheets of aluminum that can then be used to make more soda cans. Tell your child, "Honey, since an aluminum can could be recycled forever, why would we want to throw it away or litter our roads, parks, or rivers with it? Besides, think what would happen if each kid in your school threw away just one can every day on the school playground. You'd have hundreds of cans in just one week. What a mess, and what a waste!"

If your youngster asks why plastic cups can't be thrown in the lake, explain that plastic is not biodegradable. That means it will *never* decay; it's permanent garbage. Not only that, but if he throws it in the lake, it floats and looks like food to some of the animals who live in water. For example, a turtle could eat the plastic and then might not be able to dive for any food again because the plastic would make him float. It would clog up his system and he'd starve to death.

When your child learns about unsightly litter and the hazards it can create for animals, he might ask what he should do when he sees another child littering. Let him know he can good-naturedly remind the other child, "Billy, don't throw that paper on the ground. That's littering!" If Billy won't cooperate, remind your child that he could pick up Billy's trash and feel good about his contribution to keeping the ground clean and uncluttered.

2. IS HUNTING BAD?
Isn't hunting a sport like tennis?

If you are pro-hunting, simply tell a young child, "Yes, Colin, I think hunting is fine so long as hunters follow the rules. There are laws about which animals can be hunted, what time of the year they can be hunted, and how many of those animals a hunter can kill." If you are against hunting, you could say something like "No, Colin, I don't believe in hunting animals. I believe that animals have the same right to live that we do."

For your older child let her know that the controversy is more complicated. For thousands of years humans have hunted animals for food, fur, and skins. Many people think hunting is fine so long as the animal is eaten or the hide or fur is used for clothing. The problem is that some people hunt the animal to have a prize to hang up in their den, to use a part of the animal for some high-cost fashionable item (such as ivory from elephant tusks), or just to see if they can kill it.

Let your youngster know there are many hunters who believe in killing animals only for food. And to make sure some endangered species aren't killed or that too many animals of one kind aren't killed even for food, there are laws that regulate the number and type of animals hunters are allowed to kill. Hunters also point out that many animals starve to death and that hunting a certain number of an overpopulated species is actually more humane than having the animals suffer from starvation.

Folks who believe that hunting for food is all right point out that many folks who are against hunting still eat fish, chicken, and meat purchased at the supermarket. They feel that if a person is against hunting, he should be a strict vegetarian. But there are many people who do eat animals from the supermarket who still do not believe in killing animals in the wild.

A basic point you want your child to understand is that there's a difference between what can be considered legitimate use of animals and blatant disregard and misuse of them. The argument of course revolves around whether or not there is a legitimate reason for hunting.

If your child asks if hunting is a sport, let her know that it is considered by many to be a sport, but not in quite the same way as football or tennis. In most sports all parties agree to enter into the event. In hunting, the animal has no choice about participating. Also, in hunting, as opposed to tennis, for example, the shots are never returned!

3. WILL I GET CANCER IF I PLAY IN THE SUN?
Why are holes in the ozone bad for us?

Although you'll probably teach your child to use a sunscreen to keep her from getting sunburned, she'll eventually hear about the potential of getting skin cancer from the sun. Help her understand that young people don't usually get skin cancer, but that protecting herself from the sun is necessary to keep herself from being at risk for skin cancer when she's much older. A little too much sun on one particular day isn't going to mean she's doomed to develop skin cancer, but repeated sunburns will increase her risk of developing it much later on in her lifetime.

To explain why sunscreens are necessary, you'll need to explain about the ozone. Tell your youngster, "Way up in the sky, above the air we breathe, is a layer of gas called ozone. It helps block out the harmful rays of the sun, letting the rays that are good for us shine down on the earth. Unfortunately many man-made gases (from air conditioners, aerosol sprays, refrigerators, etc.) are floating up into the atmosphere and making holes in the ozone. Scientists are worried about the harmful rays of the sun, which come through these holes and damage the earth and the people who live here."

When your child asks how the holes in the ozone are bad for her, give her an example: "Trish, that's why people need to use a sunscreen if they go out in the sun or spend time at the beach. The sunscreen protects your skin from those harmful rays. If a person spends a lot of time in the sun during her life and her skin absorbs those rays, she can get skin cancer. The more holes in the ozone, the more harmful rays we have to protect ourselves from."

4. MOM, IS IT BAD TO WEAR FURS?
How come people get so upset about fur coats when shoes are made from animals too?

Tell your youngster that people have been wearing animal skins and furs since the days of the caveman. However, many people no longer buy or wear natural fur because they don't approve of killing exotic animals to get it. These folks might acknowledge that people in some societies must kill animals in order to have hide and fur for warm clothes but that the furs worn in our society to make expensive coats are not necessities but only decorative luxuries. These people believe that animals should not be killed unnecessarily.

Once you explain the controversy, you'll naturally want to tell your child what you believe. It's not enough to give your child both viewpoints and leave him hanging; he needs to know what you think and why you think it.

An older child might ask why people get upset about fur coats and not shoes, since leather for shoes often comes from animals that are slaughtered for food. Since the animal is killed to eat anyway, isn't using the hide for shoes a way to make good use of all parts of the animal? Explain that getting fur for coats and exotic leather for shoes usually involves killing an animal specifically to obtain its high-priced hide or fur, and the meat of the animal is thrown away. Since the fur and hides are used for adornment rather than for any utilitarian purpose, many people object to this practice.

5. IF COMPANIES KNOW IT'S BAD TO DUMP CHEMICALS, WHY DO THEY DO IT?

When your child hears about companies polluting our environment by dumping harmful chemicals into it, she might ask why these companies don't stop this practice. Explain that those companies probably would have to spend large amounts of money to change their way of disposing of the chemicals. The more money they spend, the less money they can keep for profit. That is what makes them reluctant to stop doing what they're doing: "Honey, many people will say they believe in a cause until they have to spend money to support it."

Of course in some cases the businesses might not have the money available to make the changes. In many cases, however, they just don't want to cut back on their profits.

Tell your child there are regulations being created that will eventually force companies to stop polluting the environment. However, regulations take time to enforce, and there are people who object to them. You might suggest that you and your child look for articles in the newspaper that present arguments on both sides of this question. Or you might encourage your youngster to write a letter of protest to a company that is polluting his city or town.

6. WILL SOMETHING BAD HAPPEN TO ME IF I EAT THIS PEACH WITHOUT WASHING IT?
Can I get sick from swimming in a polluted lake?
How do I know the water in the pool (lake) isn't polluted?

When your child hears about pesticides being used on fruit and vegetables in the supermarket, she might be afraid to eat them. Let her know it's a good idea to wash produce before eating it, not only to remove traces of pesticide but also because lots of people's hands have handled it getting it into the bin at the store. Even organically grown produce that has no pesticide should be washed before it's eaten. Let her know we all need to eat fruits and vegetables as part of a healthy diet, and our risk of getting sick from the pesticides is very small compared to the many benefits we get from eating these foods, especially if we wash them well.

But what about swimming in a polluted lake? Let your youngster know that this can be dangerous due to the bacteria that contaminate the water. Realize that he might think such concerns are silly since he'd be swimming and not drinking the water, so explain that when a person goes swimming, he's likely to swallow small amounts of water without even realizing it. Also, oil and chemicals in polluted water can irritate a swimmer's skin or cause other diseases.

Your child might ask how she can tell whether or not a swimming pool, lake, or other body of water is polluted. Tell her that the water in places used for public swimming is usually regularly tested for pollution. This is why it's important to swim only in water where swimming is specifically allowed. Polluted water usually has NO SWIMMING signs posted, but even if no sign is posted, it's safest never to swim unless you know for *certain* that the water is safe for swimming. Also, a person should not swim or play in water that is obviously dirty looking or filled with litter, no matter what the signs say.

7. WHERE WILL THE ANIMALS GO IF WE CUT DOWN THE FOREST?
If the animals are going to die, why can't we save them?

When forests are destroyed, animals who live in them can't survive unless they can find another natural habitat. There's no getting around this fact.

Explain to your child that the real dilemma about cutting down forests is that people need the wood from the trees to make buildings and houses. Wood is also used to make many other items, such as paper. Not only that but cutting down, preparing, and using wood provides many jobs for people. So you have the problem of leaving the forests alone so that the animals can live versus cutting down the forests so that people can have jobs, homes, paper, and other wood by-products.

If your child asks why we can't save the animals, let her know that most animals cannot survive unless they can live in their own natural environment. A few can be placed in zoos, which try to re-create a natural habitat for them, but there are not enough zoos to handle all the animals.

People who are worried about the forests want laws to be passed that will make sure the trees that are cut down are replaced with new seedlings. However, a forest can't be replanted quickly enough to save the animals living in it. Conservationists are involved in capturing and transporting forest animals to other areas where the animals' natural habitat has been preserved.

8. Why Doesn't Everybody Recycle?

When your child learns about recycling, especially if you're doing it at home, he might ask why everybody doesn't do it. Let him know there are several reasons. First, habits are very hard to break. People have been used to throwing all their trash into one container for years and years. Now they're being asked to take the time to separate it into paper, plastic, aluminum, glass, and so forth. Old habits can be hard to break, and that means change takes a long time.

Second, even if people are willing to change the way they save their garbage, in many cities there is no pickup for recycled garbage. People have to take their garbage to a recycling center. This takes time and effort, and many folks just aren't willing to do it.

Third, some cities don't even have a recycling center. To build one takes money. So lack of money becomes an obstacle to recycling, especially in small towns.

Fourth, many people are still ignorant about the need for recycling. After all, it's still a pretty new idea for most people.

You might want to encourage your child to take on recycling as one of her special home chores. She can be responsible for setting up containers for aluminum, paper, and plastic and for taking out the bins for pickup (or reminding you when it's time for a trip to the recycling center).

Let your youngster know that kids can have a great impact on the adults around them by educating the grown-ups about recycling. Many parents have ended up recycling because a child brought home information from school that convinced them the future of planet Earth could be at stake.

MORE SUGGESTIONS

1. Encourage your school to start a recycling program. Kids (and their parents) learn best by doing! Or to take research field trips that might teach kids about environmental issues. Cleanup days at parks can also be a rewarding class outing.

2. Plant a tree with your child. This event gives you a marvelous opportunity to teach her all the many ways trees help the earth and the people on it.

3. Become a member of an environmental group as a family—or let your child join one. Some of these organizations have special interests, such as saving animals or preserving the ocean. Others are more general and are involved in many issues having to do with the future of our environment.

13
Spirituality

WHETHER OR NOT YOU HAVE SPECIFIC RELIGIOUS BELIEFS, YOU MIGHT WANT your child to believe in something greater than herself or any other human being. Whether you call it God, Spirit, Fate, the Life Force, Mother Nature, or simply Goodness, such a concept conveys that there's a supreme power that brings order to all of creation.

Since young children are so literal, it's difficult for them to grasp an abstract notion like God. In our society most youngsters will envision God as a large, bearded grandfatherly figure who sits in the sky, sort of like Santa Claus minus the red suit. Consequently you have the difficult job as a parent of helping your child grasp an infinite intangible in a finite, three-dimensional world where people are used to believing something only if they can see, touch, hear, taste, or smell it.

While we grown-ups can be cynical and want to have things "proven" to us, children typically have no problem with faith. They accept their parents' ideas as fact, so your teachings about God—or the nonexistence of God—will be accepted by your child at face value just like any other belief you share with her. It's in the preteen and teen years that she might actively begin to question your values and ideas.

You'll be best able to answer your child's questions about God and religion if you've clarified your own beliefs as much as possible. Naturally if you believe in God, you'll tell her that. If you're in the process of questioning your faith, it's best to save discussion of your own doubts until your child is older. If you do not believe in God, you'll be honest with your child about that fact.

Know that a belief in a supreme power can help your youngster feel loved in spite of her mistakes or adversities, boosting her feelings of self-worth. It also helps her understand that she isn't the center of the universe, but rather an important part of a very large whole.

Even if you do not have religious or spiritual beliefs, consider exposing these concepts to your child just as you'd want to educate her about various countries, cultures, and artistic pursuits. Invite her to find the common threads in the many different religious belief systems, stressing the importance of tolerance for other points of view as well as the value of peaceful coexistence between them. Let her know that spirituality comes in many forms and is a highly personal matter. The man or woman who walks along a riverbank appreciating the delicate balance of nature might be just as spiritual—or more so—as the person who goes to church or synagogue on a regular basis.

1. WHAT IS GOD?
   Where is God?

Your child will naturally have trouble grasping the difficult concept of an omniscient presence that is infinite. You'll need to explain that God probably isn't a man sitting up in the sky, but that many people envision God as a force or a spirit that cannot be seen or touched: "Honey, there are some things that are real but that cannot be seen, heard, or touched. For example, you know I love you, and you can feel that I love you, but you can't really see my love like you can see my face or a flower. God is the energy of love. Wherever love is, God is there."

For an older child you might use the analogy of a seed: "Marie, there is a life force that exists in a seed that makes it into a flower. You could cut the seed open, but you couldn't see that life force. Yet you know it's there because the seed does grow into a flower. God is like that life force. We cannot see God, but we can see God's creations."

If you believe God is a part of everyone and everything, you might use the analogy of the ocean: "Sean, a drop of water from the ocean is not the ocean, which is far bigger, but that drop is made up of the ocean. God is like the ocean, and you and I are like the drops; we're not God, but a part of God is within us."

You might also want your youngster to come to the understanding that God is a force that brings order to the universe. There is a force that makes the sun, the stars, and the planets move about in a pattern, a force that brings about a balance of nature. Let her know that God is a very big idea, one that is very difficult to comprehend, even for grown-ups, and that many people have many different ideas about who, what, and where God is—and whether God exists at all.

Most children who are taught to believe in God will have about the same proportion of love, awe, trust, and/or fear toward God that they have toward their parents. While religions differ in their view of whether or not God should be feared, with a young child it's best to emphasize the loving and forgiving aspects of God so that she doesn't become frightened and guilty about her real or imagined mistakes.

If you believe in God, your child might ask where God is. Explain that since God is not a person, God doesn't live in a "place" the way people do. Because God is a force that can be anywhere and everywhere, like the wind. We know that when we see love and kindness, God is there.

2. How Do You Know There Is a God?
Why don't some people believe in God?
Is God watching me?

Tell your child that a person cannot prove that God exists the way a person would prove that a tree or a chair exists. Since God is not a tangible object or person, you cannot see, hear, touch, smell, or taste God (in the usual sense). But you can know God is there because you see God's effects, all the things God has created. This would include the sun, moon, stars, planets, mountains, oceans, animals, birds, fish, and people.

Tell your child that some people believe in God through faith because they see all these wonderful creations. But many people also come to have a personal sense of God through some experience in their life when they have a very strong feeling that God has communicated directly with them in some mystical way.

When your child asks why some people don't believe in God, tell him that God's existence cannot be scientifically proven, and for that reason some people do not believe God exists. These people might have other philosophical belief systems (such as a belief that everything that happens, happens for a reason) that do not include God as part of them. Or sometimes a person who believes in God has something so bad happen in his life that it makes him decide that there is no God. Then, too, many people don't believe in God for some or most of their lives, but then change their minds because of some experience which convinces them God is real.

If you do not believe in God and your child expresses this same belief, he might find himself the subject of ridicule by his peers. As with any other belief he holds that might not be popular, he needs calmly to assert his right to believe differently: "I know you believe in God, Tammy, but I don't. Everybody is entitled to his own opinion," or, "Tammy, you and I just believe differently about this. There really is no way to *prove* that God exists."

If your child wants to know if God is watching her, you might tell her many people think God knows everything that happens to everyone. Again, it's not like there's a little man spying on her, but more like a force in the world that is intelligent and knowing. You might want her to see this force as loving and caring rather than critical and judgmental.

3. How Come There Are So Many Religions If There Is Only One God?
   Which church is right?

Explain to your child that religion is very personal and that many people believe quite differently about it. Although disagreements about God and religion have started wars, for the most part a person's religion is a private belief that might change or expand as a person goes through life. Faith is unique to each individual; some people express it by going to church, others by a more private form of worship.

However, since the beginning of time people have been fascinated with ideas about how the world was created: "Honey, some people have tried to understand how the world began through science; others have tried to understand it with their feelings. Those who believe in a supreme power, such as God, might have called God by different names, but they were all trying to figure out the supreme force that they believe created our world."

Let your child know that even though there are many different religions around the world, most of them share common threads. In spite of their differences, they usually emphasize love, kindness, honor, mercy, and respect for all of creation.

Since your younger child usually thinks in terms of right and wrong, he might ask which church or religion is right. While you'll want to tell him why you prefer your particular spiritual beliefs, let him know that all religions involve interpretations and opinions. Since God and other spiritual matters cannot be scientifically proven, nobody truly has a final, definitive answer. You might want to add, "Honey, there are many paths to truth; the important thing is to be on a path and to respect other people's belief systems."

4. WILL GOD ANSWER MY PRAYERS?
   I keep praying that Uncle Max will get better. Why doesn't God listen?
   If I ask God for a computer game, will God bring me one?

Explain to your child that prayer is simply a way for him to tell God what's on his mind. He can tell God what he's happy and thankful about, what worries him, and he can ask for God's help. "But what you need to understand, Mike, is that God might not answer your prayers in just the way you want or expect. You're just telling God the way you'd *like* it to be, but it's not that you're giving God an order. God will decide what is best for you." Or, "Arnie, God doesn't make anything happen, bad or good. God just gives us the strength to weather life's difficulties."

Tell your child that it's hard to know sometimes if God has answered a prayer, especially if what she's asking for doesn't happen. For instance, if she asks God for a horse and doesn't get one, she might think God didn't listen. But God might know that a horse is not what she really needs, but rather that she's really lonely and needs more friends. So God might send along a new friend for her instead of a horse.

If your child prays for someone who's ill to get well and the person gets worse or dies, he'll have a difficult time understanding why God would let this happen. Explain to him that no one really understands why God lets something bad happen to a particular person, but we have to accept that God has a reason that we can't understand: "Larry, I don't know why God wanted Uncle Mark to be with him in heaven right now, but I believe God had a reason." Your youngster might want some examples of such a reason, so you might tell him, "Well, maybe God needed Uncle Mark to do something else in the next dimension" (if you believe in an afterlife or reincarnation), or, "Maybe God took Uncle Mark because Uncle Mark had finished his work here," or, "Honey, it was just part of God's plan. We might never understand it."

5. WHERE IS HEAVEN?
   How do I know if I'll go to heaven when I die?
   Is our kitty in heaven now?
   Are there really angels?

Tell your child that nobody really knows for sure where—or if, depending on your beliefs—heaven is, but when a person is in heaven, he is with God and has total peace of mind. If he's old enough to understand, you could even explain that heaven might not be a "place" in the usual sense, but a state of consciousness that exists whenever people are with God after they die. Because heaven is filled with God's presence, it is a beautiful, loving place where there is no pain or conflict.

Your child might want to know how she can be sure she'll go to heaven when she dies. Realize that she might be asking this question because she is afraid she's done something bad or is worried that she might make mistakes in the future. Reassure her by letting her know that God is forgiving and knows that all of us make mistakes: "Honey, you are a wonderful little girl and will grow to become the wonderful person God wants you to be. God knows what's in a person's heart, and God forgives our mistakes if we ask for forgiveness. I'm sure you'll go to heaven when you die."

Your child might ask if a pet who has died will go to heaven the way people do. Tell her that God loves animals, too, and takes care of their spirits after they die. Since God is taking care of them, they are in heaven.

Since children often hear that angels live in heaven, your youngster might ask if you think angels really exist. If you don't believe in angels, tell your child so. If you do, explain them as nonhuman spirit beings who live invisibly in another dimension watching over us. You might want to elaborate that God gives each of us a special angel, called a guardian angel, to look after us and help us.

6. MARK SAYS THERE'S A DEVIL. IS HE RIGHT?
   Where is hell?
   Will I go to hell for hitting my brother?

Obviously your answer to the question of whether or not the devil exists will depend on whether you do or don't believe in the devil. However, realize that your child is not asking this as a theological issue so much as out of a desire for reassurance that he isn't going to be "taken over" by some evil force that will turn him into a bad person. Reassure him that if he loves God, he doesn't have to worry about the devil.

If you don't believe in the devil, then how do you explain the existence of evil to your child? You might say something like, "Steve, God gives all of us the free will to choose good or evil. God wants us to choose the good, but some people don't. Those people might be angry, hurt, confused, or have bad luck, so they follow a path that we call evil."

If your child wants to know about hell, let her know that some people think there's a place called hell where evil people go to after they die; other people think there is no such place because God wouldn't let there be one, or because they don't believe in concepts of heaven or hell. Explain that sometimes people create a type of "hell" during their life by making bad choices, hurting others, and hurting themselves.

Reassure your youngster that children do not go to hell, if there is one. If a child deliberately does something that results in hurt to another person, he can be forgiven for his wrongdoings by loving God and asking for God's help.

7. WHY DOES GOD LET BAD THINGS HAPPEN?
   Why did God let Mommy get killed in that car wreck?
   How come God lets some kids be born sick or deformed?

Your child might naturally wonder why a loving God would allow tragic events such as accidents, natural disasters, poverty, diseases, and war to happen. For the simplest explanation you might say, "Molly, it's a very hard thing to understand, even for grown-ups. But I have faith that God has a reason for everything, even if we don't understand it."

If your child experiences the death of someone close to her who did not die of "old age," she might question how God could let such a terrible thing happen. Again, explain that you don't understand the reason why it happened either. You might tell her, "All you can do is have faith that God had some reason for taking that person and that the person is at peace," or, "Maybe God had nothing to do with it. God is just here to support you," depending upon your beliefs. Realize that your child might be thinking she's responsible for the death in some way, so let her know that the person's dying had nothing to do with whether your child did something bad or good (see Chapter 5, "Sickness/Death").

When your youngster asks why God would let some children be born sick or deformed, explain that such children serve as important teachers to the rest of us. Give her a few examples: "Honey, a child who is deformed might become a wonderful painter or writer, teaching us all that the way a person's body looks doesn't have anything to do with the happiness, intelligence, beauty, or talent that can lie inside it," or, "People who have to overcome handicaps teach the rest of us a lot about patience, determination, and courage." In the case of children who are never able to function well in any area of living, tell your child that those children can teach us about unconditional love, which means loving someone without any expectation that they can do something for us in return for our love.

An older youngster might understand that even a tragedy can have some positive outcome. Accidents, illness, and death reinforce the value of life and teach us to appreciate the blessings in our lives.

8. WHAT'S A SOUL?
If there's a life after death, will I be able to see and touch things after I die?
Will I get to see Grandpa again when I die?
What's reincarnation?

Tell your child that some people believe that a soul is the part of each one of us that lives on after our body dies. It's not a part of us that can be seen or touched; it is more like an invisible spirit. In other words we are all spiritual beings housed in human bodies.

If you believe in an afterlife, your child might want to know if that life will be like the one he knows now. Will he be able see, hear, and touch things? Let him know that nobody really knows what life after death is like or if it exists, but most people who believe in an afterlife assume it will be different from this dimension and that we are not likely to have bodies as we know them now.

As for the question of seeing relatives and loved ones in the hereafter, most people who believe in afterlife assume that souls or spirits have a way of recognizing one another. In that sense everyone is together again after death.

When your child asks about reincarnation, explain that many people think souls live many lifetimes. In other words after a person dies, her soul can be reborn in the body of another person. People who believe in reincarnation think that a soul makes a journey through its many lives to perfect itself to the point where it can be eternally with God, learning important lessons along the way from each lifetime.

Sometimes children who are taught the concept of reincarnation become frightened that they will come back as a type of person they don't want to be (such as a murderer or a poor, starving child in an undeveloped country). Part of the reincarnation theory, however, is that a soul chooses the kind of life experience it will have when it comes back in human form. Knowing it is her own soul's choice is reassuring to the child.

As with all these questions about spirituality, reassure your youngster that she doesn't have to try to figure everything out while she's a child. As she matures, her own belief system will take shape, not only from the ideas she learns as she's growing up but also from the many life experiences she will have.

MORE SUGGESTIONS

1. Whatever your spiritual beliefs, talk about them with your child so that they become a natural part of his daily life (in addition to something he'll discuss in church or synagogue).

2. Participate in religious celebrations, rituals, or holidays with your child. If you are not a member of an organized religious group, teach your child your own spiritual symbols and family rituals (meditation, reading the Bible and other spiritual works, blessings, prayer, etc.).

3. When the subject of other people's religions or spiritual orientations comes up, help your child see the similarities as well as the differences between these beliefs and your own. Your child is much more likely to develop spiritual values if he sees the common threads that are important to so many different groups across our planet.

Suggested Readings

FOR PARENTS

Babcock, Dorothy E., and Terry D. Keepers. *Raising Kids OK.* New York: Avon, 1977.

Dodson, Fitzhugh. *How to Father.* New York: New American Library, 1978.

————. *How to Parent.* New York: New American Library, 1971.

Dreikurs, Rudolf. *Coping with Children's Misbehavior.* New York: Hawthorn Books, 1972.

Dreikurs, Rudolf, and Loren Grey. *A Parent's Guide to Child Discipline.* New York: Hawthorn Books, 1970.

Eckler, James D. *Step by Step-Parenting.* Morton Grove, Ill.: Betterway Publications, 1988.

Elkind, David. *The Hurried Child.* New York: Addison-Wesley Publishing Co., 1988.

Faber, Adele, and Elaine Maglish. *How to Talk So Kids Will Listen and Listen So Kids Will Talk.* New York: Avon, 1982.

Gardiner, Richard A. *The Parents Book About Divorce.* New York: Creative Therapeutics, 1977.

————. *Understanding Children: A Parent's Guide to Child-Rearing.* New York: Creative Therapeutics, 1979.

Ginot, Haim G. *Between Parent and Child.* New York: Avon, 1971.

Gordon, Thomas. *Parent Effectiveness Training.* New York: Peter H. Wyden, 1973.

Grollman, Earl A. *Explaining Death to Children.* New York: Beacon Press, 1969.

Ingersol, Barbara. *Your Hyperactive Child.* New York: Doubleday, 1988.

Patterson, Gerald R. *Living with Children.* Champaign, Ill.: Research Press, 1968.

Patterson, Gerald R., and Leslie Becker. *Parents Are Teachers.* Champaign, Ill.: Research Press, 1971.

Popkin, Michael. *Active Parenting.* San Francisco, Calif.: Harper & Row, 1987.

Schaefer, Charles E., and Howard L. Millman. *How to Help Children with Common Problems.* New York: Van Nostrand Reinhold Company, 1981.

Tureki, Stanley K., and Leslie Tonner. *The Difficult Child.* New York: Bantam, 1989.

FOR CHILDREN

Banish, Roslyn. *A Forever Family.* New York: HarperCollins Publishers, 1992.

Bryan, Mellanie, and Robert Ingpen. *Lifetimes.* New York: Bantam Books, 1983.

Cole, Joanna. *The New Baby at Your House.* New York: Mulberry Books, 1985.

Delton, Judy. *My Mother Lost Her Job Today.* Chicago: Albert Whitman & Company, 1980.

Gardiner, Richard A. *The Boys and Girls Book About Divorce.* New York: Creative Therapeutics, 1977.

———. *The Boys and Girls Book About Step-Families.* New York: Creative Therapeutics, 1983.

Girard, Linda W. *My Body Is Private.* Morton Grove, Ill.: Albert Williams & Company, 1984.

Grollman, Earl A. *Talking About Death: A Dialogue Between Parent and Child.* New York: Beacon Press, 1991.

Livingston, Carole. *Why Was I Adopted?* New York: Carol Publishing Group, 1990.

Madaras, Lynda. *What's Happening to My Body? Book for Boys.* New York: Newmarket Press, 1984.

———. *What's Happening to My Body? Book for Girls.* New York: Newmarket Press, 1988.

Mayle, Peter. *What Am I Doing in a Stepfamily?* New York: Carol Publishing Group, 1992.

———. *What's Happening to Me?* New York: Carol Publishing Group, 1990.

———. *Where Did I Come From?* New York: Carol Publishing Group, 1973.

Sharmat, Marjorie W. *Mitchell Is Moving.* New York: Aladdin Books, 1978.

Stein, Sara B. *Making Babies.* New York: Walker & Company, 1974.

Varley, Susan. *Badger's Parting Gifts.* New York: Mulberry Books, 1984.

Index